BUS

ALLEN COUNTY PUBLIC LIBRARY

A
D

D0517245

547 WAYS TO BE FUEL SMART

Every tip will pay off in lower fuel bills and more comfortable living

ROGER ALBRIGHT

STOREY BOOKS

Schoolhouse Road
Pownal, Vermont 05261

The mission of Storey Communications is to serve our customers by publishing practical information that encourages personal independence in harmony with the environment.

Edited by Larry Shea
Cover design by Leslie Constantino
Text design by Mark Tomasi
Text production by Erin Lincourt
Indexed by Pamela Van Huss

Copyright © 2000, 1990, 1978 by Storey Communications, Inc.

All rights reserved. No part of this book may be reproduced without written permission from the publisher, except by a reviewer who may quote brief passages or reproduce illustrations in a review with appropriate credits; nor may any part of this book be reproduced, stored in a retrieval system, or transmitted in any form or by any means — electronic, mechanical, photocopying, recording, or other — without written permission from the publisher.

The information in this book is true and complete to the best of our knowledge. All recommendations are made without guarantee on the part of the author or Storey Books. The author and publisher disclaim any liability in connection with the use of this information. For additional information, please contact Storey Books, Schoolhouse Road, Pownal, VT 05261.

547 Ways to Be Fuel Smart was previously published under the title *547 Tips for Saving Energy in Your Home*. All of the information in the previous edition was reviewed and revised for this new text.

Storey Books are available for special premium and promotional uses and for customized editions. For further information, please call Storey's Custom Publishing Department at 1-800-793-9396.

Printed in the United States by Capital City Press
10 9 8 7 6 5 4 3 2

Library of Congress Cataloging-in-Publication Data

Albright, Roger, 1922-
    547 ways to be fuel smart / by Roger Albright.
        p. cm.
    ISBN 1-58017-369-1 (alk. paper)
    1. Dwellings—Energy conservation. 2. Conservation of natural resources.
I. Title: Five hundred and forty-seven ways to be fuel smart. II. Title.

TJ163.5.D86 A435 2000
696—dc21   00-049252

Contents

Introduction

We can save money and live a more comfortable life by being fuel smart. Simple changes can save enough energy to make a big difference in your bottom line. This book will provide information and guidance on some practical and affordable things you can do to your home and in your daily life to save energy.

First, a quick lesson on how your home loses heat.

→ **Conduction:** Hold a glass filled with hot water in your hand. The outer surface of the glass feels warm. Heat is transferred from the water to your hand through the glass by conduction. So long as the water is warmer than your hand, heat will conduct through the glass. Nothing actually passes through the glass; instead, fast-moving molecules bump against their neighbors, making them heat up. In the same way, heat passes through walls.

A material that slows the flow of heat can be used as insulation. Most insulation materials work in basically the same way. They trap air in tiny pockets and prevent air currents from quickly taking the heat away.

The ability of a material to stop heat flow and act as insulation is indicated by its "R-factor." The higher the R-factor, the better the insulation. When buying insulation, always look for the highest R-factor. You must also consider other factors: cost, ease of installation, durability, flammability, and water resistance.

→ **Convection:** Hold a stick of incense next to a cold window. Which way does the smoke go? Down. Hold it next to a warm radiator. The smoke rises. The smoke is riding on currents of air. Because cold air falls, near a chilly window air currents go down. Conversely, near a radiator air rises. Air currents carry heat from one place to another.

On windy days, a thin film of air surrounding our bodies is swept away by the wind. We lose heat. Our bodies heat another layer of air. Again, it is swept away. This is another example of convection.

Homes lose heat through convection. Heated air constantly rises inside your home and is swept away through holes or cracks. Cold air enters, especially near the floor. Convection in the home is often felt as a draft.

➡ **Radiation:** Do you feel cold when you stand next to a large picture window on a cold winter day? Does your front feel warm and your back feel cold when you stand facing a hot woodstove? In each case, radiation is at work. Warm surfaces radiate or lose their heat to cold surfaces. You are radiating your heat to that cold window. The woodstove radiates its heat to the room. Radiators work through radiation and convection. The surface area radiates heat, and air currents carry it into the room.

We will be using these concepts as we guide you through ways to save energy. It is helpful to know how heat energy is transferred when you're trying to reduce heat loss.

Note: The chapters on home weatherization cover mostly heating. If you live in a region where it is hot in the winter and even hotter in the summer, these same practices will help you save on your cooling bill. Sections of chapter 3 and chapter 11 focus on cooling.

Your Home Is a System

Over the past twenty years, we have learned that the house is a system. If you do something to one area, you will probably affect another area. That's why you need to consider humidity, moisture, and air quality when you are contemplating energy improvements.

I will point out how these systems interact in the discussion of each topic. For example, condensation relates to the degree of insulation. Warm air can hold a lot of moisture. When the air cools down, it can hold less moisture. On hot, humid summer days, have you ever noticed water dripping down the outside of a cold glass of lemonade? As the warm air comes into contact with the cold glass, the water vapor in the air loses temperature and is converted to water. The moisture is known as condensation.

In your home, warm air is conducted through glass, walls, floors, and ceilings to the outdoors. When you weatherize your home you want to make sure that the warm air, as it cools, does not condense in your walls, on your windows, or inside the insulation. One way to prevent condensation is by installing a vapor barrier toward the heated space. The vapor barrier prevents the moisture from leaving the heated space.

The key to success is understanding the way all the little things you do around the house add up to the big picture. The good news is that you *can* make a difference. If you apply even a fraction of the hints and tips in this book to your own home, you will see immediate cost savings in your utility bills. Perhaps even more important, you will be helping to conserve the world's energy resources.

chapter 1 ⟹ ⟹ ⟹ ⟹ ⟹ ⟹ ⟹ ⟹ ⟹ ⟹

Get Ready for Winter!

So you're standing out in front of the house taking a good look at it. Nice house. Happy memories inside. Pleasant place. You're proud of it. But even though it may be a warm haven from the troubles of the world, your house may also be leaking heat from hundreds of unseen cracks and openings.

If that's the case, your home is the enemy of your budget, the destroyer of your plans for a dream vacation, and a secret ally of your predatory fuel supplier. Action is called for.

What you strive for in your residential castle is a place that is secure from invaders. Today, the invaders threatening to steal your fortune are sneaky drafts, whistling winds, and the silent cold that comes in the dark of the night.

There are various ways to deal with chilly drafts after they get in the house, but the best way is to stop them at the threshold, so to speak, before they get inside. Your goal is to make your house a more airtight package. In most older homes you don't need to worry about getting too airtight. The average place will continue to "breathe," and there will be plenty of fresh air, even after you do your best to fill the cracks.

Filling the cracks is essentially what you're up to. Here's why. A crack just ¼-inch wide around an average door is about the same size as a hole in your wall 6 inches square. Just imagine how much cold air can rush through a gap that size.

You will need a few tools for your security effort, but none of them are expensive and all of them are easy to use. As much time as you have available is all you'll need to begin. You may not get the whole job done right away, but every part of your effort will pay off in lower fuel bills and more comfortable living.

The best time to get at it is late summer and fall. There's a nip in the morning air to give you an incentive, but it's still warm enough to comfortably work outdoors. Later on, when winter really hits, some of the things you'd like to do are difficult or impossible: Caulking and glazing compounds gum up in the cold, and patching cement won't set properly if the temperature is below freezing.

As you read this, is it already too late? Not at all. Even in the middle of December there are still things you can do this season, as well as good resolutions you can make about next year.

Here we go!

Make Your Doors Airtight

A good place to start the security check is with your outside doors. They're used many times a day all year-round and are likely to lose their tightness of fit more rapidly than windows. Even if you have storm doors, you need to check the main doors carefully.

If you can see daylight around the door when it's closed, you have a major job on your hands. You may need to reset the hinges to get a better fit. However, adding lath strips on the inside of the doorframe may cover those gaps, and then you can add weather stripping to complete the job. If you feel cold air coming through, weather stripping may be all you need.

The full weather-stripping job on an outside door should cost $10 to $15 and, with a few annual adjustments, should last about 5 years. You may even save that amount in this winter's fuel costs, which means the job is paid for in the first year. That's a better return than you get by putting your money in the bank.

Several kinds of weather stripping are available. Some are better than others. Plastic adhesive V-strips are easy to install and will last a long time, depending on how much use the door gets. When installing the adhesive-backed weather stripping, make sure to clean the surface well and reinforce the adhesive with small tacks spaced approximately every 6 inches. Wood or aluminum door kits with vinyl bulb weather stripping last longer and are slightly more expensive.

The bottom of the door is the most important place to get a good seal, and the most difficult. If your threshold is worn, a tight weather-strip job is just about impossible, and a new threshold is called for. A soft wood such as pine planking is the easiest to cut and the cheapest to buy but won't last a year in a heavily trafficked spot. Make it a hard wood like oak, or get a metal doorsill.

To make a weathertight seal, install a door sweep on the bottom of the door. Several different products are available. Most are aluminum with a vinyl sweep made to withstand light, medium, or heavy use. Automatic door sweeps cause the sweep to lift as it comes over the inside carpet.

Almost as important as the door itself is the line where the doorframe meets the house. The door is probably slammed shut more than a thousand times a year, and that can loosen the caulking around the frame. You can buy a caulking gun and some tubes of caulking

Too Dry?

Is your home too dry in the winter? When your house has the proper humidity level, you'll be more comfortable at a lower thermostat setting. Two signs of a house lacking moisture are:

1. Wooden furniture comes apart.
2. Those in the house complain of dry noses and often have head colds.

You can purchase an inexpensive hygrometer that measures relative humidity. During the winter, the comfort range is from 30 to 50 percent. Try using a humidifier or leaving the lids off pots on the stove to add moisture to the air.

compound at any hardware store. Do it. Look for a siliconized acrylic latex caulk. Many caulks come in various colors or are paintable. You'll be using the gun in a lot of other places, so it's a good investment.

You have a storm door? Good! Be sure the framing of the storm door is screwed tightly to the doorframe.

If you're installing a storm door, put a bead of caulk across the top and down both sides before you install the frame. Then with the frame screwed in place, you're sure to have a tight and permanent seal against breezes.

Do a good job on the front door, storm door and all, and you'll save $50 a year or more on your fuel bills, which makes it well worth the effort. You'll feel a lot more comfortable, too!

Stop Heat from Going out the Window

Let's check the windows. That may sound like a big chore, so here's a priority system: The west-facing windows are most likely to catch the prevailing winds, so do them first; the north-facing windows will be exposed to the coldest air, so do them second. The east-facing windows are next. Southern windows, facing the sun, are probably the least vulnerable, so they can wait till last.

➡ Can you hear your windows rattle in a heavy windstorm? Yes? Then you have an important weather-stripping job to do. Do little breezes sometimes move the curtains even when the windows are closed? Yes? Then you need both weather stripping and caulking.

Two types of products that are easy to install are rope caulk and V-seal weather stripping. The rope caulk is applied in the fall and removed in the spring. With rope caulk in place, you cannot open the window. The V-seal is applied on the window jamb and enables you to open and close the window while it is in place.

Windows Shut = Money Saved

The remodeled schoolhouse where I live has four big windows (4 feet wide by 8 feet high). I like them, but they added to my fuel bill every winter. A year or two after I moved in I realized that there was plenty of summer ventilation from other sources and that the big windows were never opened. Now they are nailed shut, their cracks are caulked, and we save money every winter.

➡ Do you have some windows that you never open? Consider shutting them with a permanent seal. Close them securely, then caulk around all four sides. Add a single-pane storm window and install a bead of caulk. The end result will be as airtight as the double-pane fixed window you call a picture window in your living room.

➡ Cracked panes in your windows, or missing putty around the glass, will let cold air leak through. Get replacement panes for cracked or broken panes and tighten up.

➡ Don't use putty, use plastic glazing compound. Putty dries out, cracks, and falls away. That's probably why the window needs to be repaired in the first place. A good glazing compound will hold up for at least 10 years before cracking and costs little more than ordinary putty. It's worth the price.

Take a glob of glazing compound and roll it between your hands until it takes the shape of a piece of rope. Then line it into the wedge made by the glass and the window frame. This makes a better seal than trying to press the compound in a dab at a time. For larger jobs, buy glazing compound in tubes, which can fit into your caulking gun.

Tricks for Using Glazing Compound

Replacing a broken window in the winter is an irritating chore because the glazing compound gets stiff and intractable. If I have that task ahead of me I tackle it with two cans of glazing compound; one in hand, and one keeping warm indoors on the windowsill. By trading them back and forth, it's possible to complete the job. If you have only one can of glazing compound, tuck it under your jacket next to your warm body to keep it workable.

➡ When installing a windowpane, you can use several kinds of glazier's tips or points to hold the glass in place. Particularly if you're up on a shaky ladder, the odds are substantial that you'll break the pane with your hammer when putting in a pane with some kinds of glazier's tips. Look for the kind with a nib sticking out. You can catch that nib with a screwdriver, tap the screwdriver handle with your hammer, and improve your chances of success considerably.

➡ Getting the glass replaced and reset is the right first step, but a window that is still rattling needs weather stripping. The most satisfactory method is to install V-strips or extruded plastic strips already shaped in a V. If you are weather-stripping many windows, you will save money if you purchase the V-strip weather stripping in 180-foot rolls. Make sure the window channels are free of dirt and grease. Clean with a damp rag before installing the V-strip. And reinforce the V-strip with small tacks.

➡️ Another area that may be leaking is around the window frame. A bead of caulking compound down both sides and at top and bottom should seal out vagrant breezes.

➡️ Have you seen those clamshell locks on many double-hung windows? Their purpose isn't just security but also to pull the sashes together to keep cold air out.

More Places You Should Seal Tightly

Sealing the cracks and holes around windows and doors definitely reduces drafts, saves you money, and keeps you more comfortable. But did you know that the winter cold may be seeping into your house in a number of other ways? Twenty to 40 percent of your heating bill may be due to cold air entering your home or warm air leaving. The technical terms are *infiltration* and *exfiltration*.

The wind blowing against one side of your house is one way in which cold air gets in and warm air is pushed out. Another way is through the "chimney effect" or "stack effect." Heated air tends to rise. This creates a difference in pressure between the top and bottom of the house. At the top, air is pushed out (exfiltration). Air is then sucked in at the bottom. In addition, combustion appliances — from boilers and furnaces to ranges and water heaters — contribute to air infiltration. As air is used during combustion it must be replaced by fresh air. Usually this fresh air is sucked into the house by whatever passageways are available.

All of the holes that were drilled for your plumbing stacks or electrical wires become pathways through which warm air can leave your home. In the attic, the partition walls become an escape route for heated air. In some houses there is nothing behind the kitchen or other cabinets to stop your heat from going into the walls and up to the attic. These paths for cold air to get into your house and warm air to get out of your house are called *bypasses.*

Finding and sealing major bypasses will definitely result in savings on your fuel bill. Now, there are specialists, often called "house doctors" or "air-sealing technicians," who are trained to find and seal these bypasses. One of their main tools is a "blower door." A blower door is basically a fan that is placed inside an exterior doorway and attached to several instruments. Its purpose is to calculate how fast air is leaving your home. With this information, the air-sealing technician can make sure that your home is not sealed too tight. You will also know just how much was accomplished through the air-sealing by comparing the blower door tests done before and after the sealing.

Will air-sealing make your house too tight? No. Will it increase the possibility of radon entering your home? No. By using the blower door, you can make sure your house will not be sealed too tightly. In addition, sealing bypasses in the attic and basement reduces the chimney effect, one of the major forces that pulls any radon from the ground right into your basement.

More and more weatherization professionals are learning about air-sealing and blower doors. Air-sealing techniques are also used extensively in new home construction.

Storm Windows Keep Out the Cold

Storm windows are an excellent buy, particularly in northern climates. Wooden frames are more efficient than metal frames because they conduct less heat from inside to outside. Fixed storm windows are less expensive than storm windows that are storm and screen combinations (tripletrack).

Many storm windows are tested for their energy performance. A high-quality storm window has an infiltration rate of less than 0.5 cubic feet per minute with a 15 miles-per-hour wind. Ask to see the manufacturer's literature on the product you buy. Make sure any window is installed well and fits snugly.

➡ In aluminum storm windows, the heavier the gauge of the metal and the deeper the tracks, or grooves, that the windows slide in, the better. Make sure they are weather stripped. Felt-pile weather stripping is most common for storms. Because metal is such a good conductor, look for a storm window with a "thermal break" to stop the flow of warm air at the metal edge of your storm window.

➡ When installing prefabricated aluminum tripletrack windows, put a bead of caulking compound between the frame of the house window and the new aluminum framing, to be sure there is a full seal to keep out drafts. Then screw in place.

➡ If full storm windows aren't practical for your house, consider plastic storm kits. Several inexpensive kits are available. Reusable plastic interior storm kits contain very clear plastic with narrow plastic strips to hold the window in place and adhere to the window frame. These can last five years or more. Another easy-to-use storm window kit is installed with a hair dryer and usually lasts one season.

➡ To seal windows from the outside, 6-mil polyethylene is sold in sheets and rolls at many hardware stores, and it will do a big job at low cost. Measure your plastic to the outer edges of the window frame, cut, then tack through ¼-inch wood slats to hold the plastic firmly to the window frame. A trim, neat job offers minimum opportunity for the wind to catch an edge and tear off the whole thing.

➡ For a house with smooth wooden siding, measure the plastic to extend beyond the window frame on all four sides and tack through the slats right into the siding.

An Old-Time Design

I remember storm windows from my youth: big, cumbersome items that were stored in the attic or the garage in the summer, if you bothered to take them down at all. One-inch holes were drilled in the bottom of the frame and covered with a hinged flap that could be opened to let in a little fresh air. All told, a very efficient design.

Check the Foundation

Masonry work should be pointed before winter, which means filling the cracks in concrete foundations and facing brickwork. Your hardware store will have ready-mix mortar for the job, and a small trowel for applying the mortar.

Mix your patching and pointing mortar in an old bucket. Cleaning it out after you're finished will be darned near impossible. If you don't finish your job in one day, hose out whatever mortar remains in the bucket; it won't keep overnight. When the job is finished you can swish the bucket out and hang it in the garage or basement.

The plank on top of your foundation wall is called a *sill plate*. If there is a crack between the sill plate and the foundation, put the caulking gun to it and fill that crack. For any crack ½-inch wide or more, use non-expanding foam. Look for an "ozone-friendly" foam that doesn't contain chlorofluorocarbons, more commonly referred to as *cfcs*.

If you have a major break in the foundation, patching may not be enough. Make a wooden frame, or form, that will cover the crack at least 2 inches on each side and at least 1 inch thick, then pour mortar into the form. Let it set at least 24 hours before removing the form.

The lapped siding used in many traditional homes can develop cracks over the years, and should be sealed with caulking. The best time to do it is just before painting. Paintable caulk is available as is caulk in a variety of colors so that you can pick out a fairly close match. Make sure that the walls have been insulated before you begin so that the siding won't have to be removed after you have sealed it.

Be sure that your cellar windows are closed tightly through the winter. Consider boarding them over for the cold season, or at least give them a double polyethylene covering.

Evergreen shrubbery around the base of your home can do much more than just serve a decorative purpose: It cuts the force of the wind at your home's most vulnerable point. Those evergreens are most important on the northern and western sides, where the winds will be strongest.

Been thinking about a toolshed or another outbuilding? You can put a metal structure up in the middle of your yard, but you'll get more for your money with a shed built right against the house. It will serve as dead-air insulation against the wall and will also stop the drafts from sneaking through that section of the foundation area.

For an attached toolshed, the best location is on a west wall; the next best is on a north wall.

If you have an outside tank for fuel oil, a framed cover for it minimizes evaporation caused by heat, tends to keep it from getting too cold for the oil to flow in subzero temperatures, and is more attractive.

Note that most local building codes wisely won't let you make an airtight structure as a cover. Be sure it is well vented so fumes won't accumulate and potentially explode.

If you have perennial flower beds at the base of your house, you may bank them with bales of hay or straw in the fall to protect the plants. Good idea. Take into account that the straw is extra insulation around the base of your house. Let your straw bed be deep and generous, but be sure to remove it in the spring or you'll run the risk of rotting the wood.

How We Use Energy

Pennsylvania State University says this is how energy is used in a home in a northern climate:

Heating of space	57.5%
Water heating	14.9%
Refrigerating	6.0%
Cooking	5.5%
Air conditioning	3.7%
Lighting	3.5%
Television	3.0%
Food freezer	1.9%
Clothes drying	1.7%
Other	2.3%

It is obvious that the big energy users in the home are heating of space and water heating, totaling 72.4 percent. This is where the most can be accomplished in saving energy.

Chapter ② ➡ ➡ ➡ ➡ ➡ ➡ ➡ ➡ ➡ ➡

Insulate Now and Save

The purpose of insulation can be stated simply: It's to keep the heat where you want it.

How Does Insulation Work?

Most insulating materials create "dead-air spaces." Heated air moves quickly, and these dead-air spaces slow down that air, so it takes longer for the warm air to mingle with the colder air outside the heated space.

What you're after is to keep the coldest air from getting in your house at the bottom and to stop the warm air from getting out through the walls or the top. In new home construction, full insulation of walls, attic, or roof is easy. In your existing home, insulating may be more difficult, but you probably can reach some of the important places.

It's important to keep the dead-air idea in mind. It's like the down jackets worn in northern climates. They will keep the body warmer than layers of solid clothing.

Good heat conductors are poor insulators. For example, a stone outer wall is low in insulation value. The same can be said for brick and concrete. Sheet metal (for the so-called tin roof), single-pane glass, stucco, and roofing shingles all fall into the same category: very little insulation value.

Lumber, composition board, and earthwalls have some insulation value, but the real winners are the expanded glass and mineral fibers you can buy as fiberglass, newspaper prod-ucts like cellulose, or rigid foam boards.

Crumpled paper and dry straw can serve that air-trapping purpose but are a fire hazard and should never be used. Dry paper can catch fire even when it is encased in a tightly sealed box made of steel ¼-inch thick.

Thorough insulation of your attic, walls, and floor can save up to 50 percent on the winter fuel bills, so we're talking about the major item in this business of saving energy. The best thing about this undertaking is that every step is profit. Even if you don't accomplish everything, each insulation area checked off on your list will be a money saver.

Start Insulating at the Top

The attic is one of the best places to save money if your insu-lation is skimpy or nonexistent.

Let's say your attic is a completely unusable space under a truss roof and isn't insulated. You have two alternatives: blan-kets of fiberglass or bags of loose fill. If possible, select the loose fill so that the rafters can be completely covered. In this way, you will minimize the bypasses created by the wood rafters. However, if the space is easy to get at and the spacing of the rafters is a standard 16 or 24 inches, fiberglass batts or rolls are a definite option. Again, the insulation will be more effective if it overlaps the rafters.

If what you're up against is a crawling job with a lot of irregular spaces, choose the bags of loose material. You may be able to rent an insulation blower. This machine will enable you to pack more insulation into each cavity. The most com-mon loose fill is cellulose, which is made from recycled news-papers and contains boron as a fire retardant.

Many attic insulation jobs can easily be do-it-yourself tasks. However, if you are also planning to insulate your walls with blown cellulose, you will probably need to hire a contractor.

How Much Insulation Do You Need?

The amount of insulation required depends on the severity of your winters, how you heat your home, and how much you can fit into the area you want to insulate. You will probably want R-38, which is equivalent to about 12 inches of insulation, in your attic.

What Else to Know before You Insulate

Don't forget about the vapor barrier. Standard insulation rolls and batts have a vapor barrier on one side. The vapor barrier should face the heated living space. With loose fill, put down 6-mil polyethylene before installing the insulation, unless the spaces are so irregular or inaccessible that such a placement is impossible.

Be sure to place insulation out far enough to cover the top of the outer wall. At the same time, be sure you don't block the vents under the eaves, if there are any. That may mean putting a piece of scrap wood or cardboard at each end of each run of loose fill to avoid plugging necessary ventilation.

In all likelihood you'll be running into light fixtures and a maze of wires up there. Unless the fixture is labeled "IC," be sure that it isn't accidentally covered during installation. Provide a minimum 3-inch clearance around the light fixtures by baffling with fiberglass batts on end. Insulation should never be in contact with bare wires. If you have any bare wires, call the electrician immediately.

The loose fill is fire resistant and can be in contact with the boxes that hold electrical connections. With batts and blankets, be sure that any paper coverings are peeled back or cut off to at least 3 inches away from any electrical junctions or fixtures.

Let's say that you have an unfinished attic, but the floor is already in place. If you're not going to use the attic, and there's no reason at all to heat it, now or in the future, your best bet will be to put insulation between the ceiling of your living space and the attic floor. If you want to do it yourself, you will need to take up the floor and put insulation between the exposed floor joists. Then you can put the floor back down again so the attic can be used as unheated storage space. You may want to get a contractor to install the insulation. The contractor will need to remove several boards, but will then be able to blow the insulation the length of the joists.

Alternatively, let's suppose the attic space is going to be used as a workshop or for some other purpose that requires heating. Then you'll want to insulate the roof.

If your roof beams are on 24-inch centers, there will be standard 6-inch fiberglass batts that will fit for insulating the roof. Make sure that air for ventilation can flow between your insulation and roof sheathing. If yours is an older house you may not have those standard spacings, in which case you'll have to cut batts to fit, or buy sheets of polystyrene foam board and cut to fit. If you use the polystyrene foam board, the way to buy is by "R" numbers. In general, these panels have high insulation value for their thickness. Again, try to insulate to R-38 if possible.

A word of caution: These foam-board panels release deadly toxic fumes if there is a fire in your home. They should be covered with Sheetrock to minimize that danger and meet most fire codes.

Some added notes on attics:

➡ When you're working in an attic, be sure you have sturdy boards to walk on and an extension light to help you see what you're doing. When walking on the floor joists, it only takes one slip to send you to the hospital, because that ceiling under you won't support you and you'll fall right through.

➡ Be careful at all times to steer clear of the roofing nails that are sticking through.

➡ The end walls can be hazardous because the nails that secure the outer siding are almost certainly sticking through. If your house has any years on it at all, those nails are dirty and rusty and likely candidates for giving you a serious infection. If you do get a puncture wound in the attic, don't mess around with it. Get to a doctor right away.

➡ Before you begin insulating, check the exposed roof areas for stains and discolorations on the wood. They indicate the presence of moisture. Be sure to find the source of moisture and assess its importance. For example, the moisture may originate from a bathroom that vents to the attic. Be sure to extend this vent to the outside. It may be due to a leaky roof. You could have a mess on your hands if you don't consider moisture as you weatherize your home. Wet insulation is ineffective and may damage your home by holding moisture and causing rot.

➡ Before insulating you should seal any places where warm air can enter your attic from your living space. Chimney channels, pipe and stack penetrations, holes made for wires and cables, and partition walls are areas you need to check.

Ventilation

When you insulate your attic, make sure that any moisture that gets into your attic is whisked to the outdoors before it can condense in your insulation or on your roof. This is the purpose of ventilation. Usually a combination of high vents and low vents is best to insure that there is adequate air flow to move the moisture effectively. Vents can be installed in the gables, eaves, or roof.

I know it seems strange to intentionally allow cold air to come into your attic, but it's better than the damage that moisture can cause. If you have a vapor barrier in place, then you will need about half as much ventilation as when there is no vapor barrier. The rule of thumb is that for every 150 square feet of attic space without a vapor barrier, or 300 square feet with a vapor barrier, you will need approximately 1 square foot of "net free area" of ventilation.

If an exhaust fan in your bathroom is venting into the attic, make sure that the air is ducted from the attic to the outside through the eaves or roof. This will help prevent warm moist air from condensing in the cold attic space where it may cause moisture problems.

Are you planning on converting your attic to living space? Perhaps the attic rooms will be able to heat themselves in the winter with what naturally rises from the house beneath, unless the attic floor is well insulated. Running heating ducts to the attic may be unnecessary.

If you expand your living space into attic rooms, avoid running water pipes up there if you can. If there are no water pipes, the rooms can be closed off when not in use, with no danger of pipes freezing and breaking.

If you have an unheated attic with flooring for storage, then there's a place for that worn carpeting when you redo the living room. Put it down on the attic floor. It may not look wonderful, but who cares? It will add a measure of insulation, and you'll be able to enjoy the luxury of wall-to-wall carpeting in the attic!

Check the door to your unheated attic and any other unheated area in the house. That door should be treated like a door to the outside: closed whenever possible and weather-stripped if needed. You can also insulate the back of this door with vinyl-backed fiberglass wrap.

When you plan to open extra rooms in the attic, be sure to include the cost of Thermopane windows or storm windows in your estimates, or the project may wind up costing you a lot more in the long run. The heat loss through attic windows can be greater because it is windier so high up.

Insulate the Walls

If yours is an older home that has never been insulated, find out whether the walls can be insulated. If you need insulation, it's easiest for a contractor to blow cellulose into the walls from the outside. The contractor will remove enough of the siding to drill a hole through the wall or clapboard. Then he will insert a hose through which cellulose will be densely packed in the wall cavity.

If you are planning to replace your present insulation or your interior walls or windows, the easiest way to insulate is to install fiberglass batts from the interior. You can remove the indoor side of the outer walls and start insulating. In an older home, you will probably have wallpaper, then plaster, then wooden lath strips, then paper, then — I hate to tell you. Inside the walls will be the dust of the centuries, augmented by whatever the mice have left behind. Have a shovel, broom, and vacuum cleaner handy. Old lead paint could be present and should be addressed at this time.

When you get into the wall you may discover that the vertical studs aren't spaced evenly, so standard insulation won't fit. You may also find braces between the studs. Those are firebreaks. They tend to slow down a fire that might otherwise run up through the walls unchecked.

When the outer wall is exposed, caulk all the gaps to the exterior. This will keep cold air from coming inside. Next, fit in the insulation as best you can, first filling in all the cracks around doors and windows. Be sure to wear protective clothing including a mask, long sleeves, goggles, and gloves. The vapor barrier should be on the warm side of the wall. If there isn't a vapor barrier on the insulation you are using, then a sheet of 4-mil polyethylene is needed. Take care not to puncture or tear the plastic because this will diminish its effectiveness.

If yours is a newer home and not insulated, the process of redoing the walls may not be as difficult. You may even be able to salvage some of the panels of Sheetrock if you are very careful when taking them down.

A final thought.

When there is any amount of insulation material to install, you'll do well to buy one super-tool. It's the staple gun. There's really no easy way to install batts or blankets of insulation without a staple gun. It's also just about essential for handling polyethylene sheets. Keep it around the house when the insulating chores are completed. You'll find yourself using it for lots of chores, and it's indispensable if you get into reupholstering a favorite chair.

Insulating in the Basement

It's sometimes a bit more complicated to figure out the best approach to insulating the basement.

Do you have an unheated basement that is used only for storage and utilities? Then you should consider insulating the basement ceiling. In effect, this is insulating the floor of your first story. After you insulate, your first floor will feel warmer and more comfortable.

Fiberglass batts are the easiest bet. Before you rush out to buy, measure. If the floor joists are spaced on 16-inch or 24-inch centers, you're in luck, because those are the standard widths for batts or rolls of insulation. The standard length for batts is 6 feet, so you can figure how many batts you're going to need for the under-floor area you're working with. The insulation should be installed flush to the ceiling to minimize air or moisture flow between the insulation and the ceiling.

Standard insulation rolls and batts have a vapor barrier on one side. Again, you want that vapor barrier to be facing the warmth, which means that in an under-floor installation the vapor barrier goes up. However, it is really difficult to get an effective and continuous vapor barrier. An equally important consideration is keeping the fiberglass fibers covered with a fire-rated material.

If you have a problem keeping the insulation in place, roll out the insulation and then tack up lengths of wire mesh or chicken wire. Metal stays are often used for this task.

A word of caution. Right now the basement may be unintentionally heated from the heating system and pipes. That under-floor insulation, if you do your job right, may leave the cellar colder. That's okay, unless there are water pipes running through the cold area. The cold water pipes may need to be wrapped to prevent freezing, and the hot water pipes should be wrapped to avoid chilling the water you are paying to heat. If you have a boiler or forced-air furnace in that space you're making colder, you will definitely need to insulate the heating pipes or heating ducts leading from the furnace.

Heating Ducts

Before insulating the heating ducts (the supply side only), check the seams between sections of both supply and return ducts to be sure they are tight. If you have any doubts, use mastic or reinforced foil duct tape. Ironically, standard duct tape is not suitable for this task. Seal the joints between sections of insulation with high-temperature vinyl tape.

Pipe Insulation

High-temperature closed-cell foam for hot-water base-board heating systems usually comes in sections 6 feet long. This foam is available for any diameter of heating-system pipe. For steam-heating systems, various sizes of high-temperature fiberglass sleeve insulation are available.

Caution: If you have steam pipes, check to see whether they are insulated with asbestos. If so, do not disturb this insulation without checking with your local health department to find out the regulations and procedures you must follow.

All you have underneath is a crawl space? Insulation will do a good job there, too. Choose a day when you are feeling calm and even tempered, and wear old clothes. An under-house crawl space will try your patience, skin your knuckles, and certainly leave you with bumps on your head and cobwebs in your ears.

Plan one trip into the crawl space just for measuring. Do a good job and make notes. Then you can cut your materials outside instead of struggling with that part of the job while you're flat on your back with spiders crawling into your collar and dust sifting into your eyes. Remember that in handling insulation such as fiberglass, you definitely must wear a mask over your nose and mouth to avoid breathing those tiny glass particles.

The materials you need are 4-mil polyethylene for a vapor barrier, R-19 fiberglass batts (the ones about 6 inches thick), and strips of wood for nailing. The boards to hold the batts in place can be scrap 1 x 2s or anything else that's handy. All you want is something strong enough to keep the insulation positioned where you need it.

How did you get into that crawl space? Through a trapdoor, an entry hatch, or a ventilation opening? Be sure any outer entry is closed tightly, weather stripped, and insulated as much as possible, or some of your effort will have been in vain.

It is important to put a layer of polyethylene on the ground to keep moisture from getting into the insulation, especially with dirt floors.

Chances are that there are some pipes leading to the kitchen sink going up an outside wall in the crawl space, and maybe some other water pipes as well. Before you leave, be sure they are well wrapped against the cold. The pipes through the crawl space may not have frozen in other years, but now that under-floor area will be colder.

The security of those exposed water pipes is doubly important if the pipes are PVC (polyvinyl chloride) or another plastic. The plastic pipes aren't as likely to burst as copper or galvanized pipes, but they are difficult to thaw if they are blocked with ice because you can't use either blowtorch heat or electric resistance treatment on them.

Ventilation in the crawl space is important to avoid wood rot and mildew problems. However, ventilation is tricky in basements and crawl spaces. Think about which is more humid — the inside or outside — and ventilate accordingly to keep moisture from building up.

On the other hand, let's say you have a basement area that is used for a variety of purposes that require it to be heated, like laundry areas, play areas, and indoor gardening efforts. Then insulating the walls is the task at hand, and it's easy, even if the existing walls are poured concrete or cinder blocks. As usual, make sure you seal all the gaps first!

On the interior of your outside walls, you'll be building another facing wall with 2 x 4s. The bottom plate will just sit on the concrete floor, not nailed to anything. The top plate can be nailed to the floor joists above it, then the vertical studs should be cut to fit snugly, or slightly force-fit, to be sure the whole works is going to stay in place.

Insulation made to fit on 24-inch centers, R-11 (about 3½ inches thick), will do well, so your vertical studs must be positioned accordingly. This isn't a bearing wall holding up house weight, so your construction can be simple.

Install the insulation from the top down to at least where the frost line is expected to be. In colder areas, that may mean running the insulation all the way down to the floor. The vapor barrier on the insulation panels should be facing the room. If the batts or rolls you buy don't have a vapor barrier, sheets of 4-mil polyethylene should be installed over the insulation after it is put in place. A continuous vapor barrier is most effective.

Cover the insulated wall with whatever suits your fancy, taking into account that cellars can be damp. Sheetrock or gypsum board can be quickly ruined if there is water on the floor, and so can plywood, unless it is exterior construction grade, which is expensive. Inexpensive wood paneling is a good bet.

If floor water may be a problem, you can run almost any kind of wallboard down to about 6 inches from the floor, then cover the gap with a board molding of 8-inch planks. Don't run the wallboard down to the floor, or it will act like a wick and draw water up to ruin your wall.

Above your new wall, between the floor joists and at both ends, will be exposed areas where insulation is needed. Place it vertically to meet the floor above and also across the top of your new wall. This won't be the most beautiful thing you've ever had in your house, but it is practical, and you won't see it at all when you finally get around to putting in a ceiling.

Chapter ③ ➡ ➡ ➡ ➡ ➡ ➡ ➡ ➡ ➡ ➡

Get Comfy Room by Room

Some people think that energy conservation can be boiled down to this: "How miserable can you stand to be?" They're afraid that saving energy will start with a plea to turn your thermostat down to 60°F and smile nobly as you shiver. Fortunately, conservation does not have to result in discomfort. With a little awareness and effort, you can trim your energy use with little sacrifice. That's what this chapter is all about.

One of the easiest ways to save fuel is through attention to your thermostat setting. Your heating system and lifestyle will determine how much flexibility you have in setting your thermostat.

The Thermostat: Your Key to Savings

Thermostats, where they are located in your home, and how you set them can be the most important factor in determining the size of your fuel bill.

➡ When you'll be out for an evening, turn down the thermostats. If you'll be away for a weekend or more, lower the thermostats to 55°F. You'll save on heating without risking a freeze-up of your water pipes.

➡ Whenever you can lower your thermostat dramatically for a few days or more, you'll save a little on the operation of the refrigerator and freezer, which won't need to work so hard to maintain their cool.

➡ How low can your thermostats be set? At our house, we've gotten accustomed to 68°F as a comfortable norm. Reduce the heat just one degree at a time and try it for a week. **Each one-degree drop for an eight-hour period reduces your fuel bill 1 percent.** Gradually, you might be able to go down three or even four degrees comfortably and save a chunk of money.

➡ Try turning down the thermostat five to ten degrees at night, and then turn it up again in the morning when the coffee is brewing. If you can get used to that, you'll save 5 to 10 percent of your heating bill.

One common myth is that when you reduce the thermostat for only a few hours it will take more heat to bring your home back up to the desired temperature. This is not so. You will save money and fuel because your heating system will not have to keep your home so warm. You will use less energy overall even when you warm up your house from a cooler temperature.

➡ For greater ease and comfort, install a programmable set-back thermostat. They are available for most gas- and oil-fueled central heating systems. In this way, you can have the heat turned up before you get up in the morning and lowered just as you get into bed. You may not even notice that you are setting back your thermostat. Most of these thermostats come with two setbacks. Therefore, you can also set back the thermostat for the hours when people are in school or at work.

➡ Some setback thermostats have different setbacks for weekends. If you frequently forget to setback your thermostat, the programmable setback thermostats will be a great investment. Even if you are already pretty good at remembering, these devices can frequently enable you to set back the thermostat a few extra degrees, providing you with additional savings.

➡ If you heat with electricity, you can take advantage of the individual room thermostats that make it possible to shut off unused rooms and to have cool settings in some rooms and warmer settings in others. Using this feature of electric heat will definitely reduce your fuel bills. If you have a thermostat that controls a relatively large area, you should still consider a setback thermostat. You will need an electrician for this installation.

➡ Do you need to talk yourself into a lower thermostat setting? Here's an argument. Your plants are healthier in the cooler air. The health of your plants isn't in the same league with your personal comfort? All right, *you'll* be healthier in the cooler air. Your body will burn a few more calories keeping you warm, thereby helping you to lose weight and improve your general health. Besides, if you've already insulated and tightened your home, you will probably be just as comfortable at lower temperatures.

➡ When it's time to open the windows for a little fresh air in the spring, remember to turn down the thermostats. Those cool breezes that feel so good will send your furnace on a fuel-burning rampage unless the thermostats are reset.

➡ Planning a party? Turn the thermostats down. Each guest is the equivalent of a 175-watt heater, and a large group will warm up the place without the furnace or the heating units in operation.

Curtains Help to Insulate

By closing curtains and shades at night, you can slice into your heating bill. Your draperies will be more effective in reducing heat loss if they are heavy or lined fabric.

Pull them back during the day, of course, for light and heat. In fact, it's best to install your drapery rods over the wall past each end of the windows. That way you can pull the drapes all the way off the windows and receive the fullest benefits of light and heat during daylight hours, especially from south-facing windows.

If you need new draperies, consider buying insulating window shades; these are typically made of fabric with special insulating qualities. Another desirable feature is an edge seal to keep any drafts from coming through your windows.

Are you on a low budget? For an unusual decorative touch, hang old patchwork quilts as window draperies. They'll be heavy enough to do a good job, are easy to hang, and will certainly be interesting. Check your local thrift shop.

How to Save Heat — and Money

A new door here, new carpeting there, and a change in habits for all members of the family. These things can add up to big savings of energy and money.

→ Don't leave the room without closing the closet door. There's no need to spend hard-earned money heating storage spaces. Clothes you're going to wear can be taken out the night before into the warmth of the room. Be your own valet and save money.

→ Take those beautiful Oriental throw rugs off the floor and hang them on the walls where people can see and enjoy them, and where they will serve as additional insulation.

→ Carpeting on floors, even in bathrooms and kitchens, is a heat-saver and comfort-maker. Durable carpeting is available that is quite practical for any location. In the bathroom, particularly, stepping out of the tub onto a cozy carpet is much nicer than bracing your toes for cold tiles. The practical advantage is that a bathroom thermostat can be set much lower without any discomfort.

→ Is there a doorway between the first and second floors of your home, or on the way up into the attic? If not, it may make sense to put one in. Stairwells act like chimney flues, conducting heat to the top of the house where you may need it less. A door may be easy to install and will tend to keep the heat downstairs where you need it.

→ Time for school? Make a habit of getting all the kids out the door at once each day, instead of opening and closing the door for each one.

→ Think about using an outdoor doghouse. Remember, your pup's ancestors lived outdoors for centuries, and he can adapt to being outdoors all year-round, unless he happens to be one of the few tropical breeds, like Chihuahuas. The

wintertime advantage to you is no more opening and closing the door umpteen times a day to let him in and out —
and no more heat lost with each opening. And with the dog
outdoors, you may spend less time with the vacuum cleaner humming to pick up dog hairs.

➡ Make sure your thermostat is located on an interior wall,
away from drafts. You don't want your thermostat to call
for heat every time the door opens!

➡ Two sets of doors at the principal entryway make a convenient foyer for putting on boots in winter and also cut heat
loss as people go in and out.

➡ Do you have a game room with a Ping-Pong table? Close it
off with a well-fitting door and let it be cooler than the rest
of the house. The action of the game will work to keep the
players warm.

➡ Planning a home workshop? Since the room will not be
used regularly, keep it off the main heating system and let it
be cool between uses. Warm it with a separate heater or a
small woodstove.

➡ Having your garage attached to your house is convenient in
many ways, but be sure to have a separate door for going in
and out to the yard or driveway. Opening the big garage
door is like taking off the side of your house, and it costs
plenty in lost heat.

➡ A rug in the children's play area gives more warmth for
playing on the floor than wood or tile. Indoor-outdoor

carpets made of synthetic yarns will take a lot of punishment and are quite stain-resistant.

➡ Go for soft, warm colors in the north rooms where direct sunlight is not available to cheer things up. You'll be surprised at the effect color has on how comfortable you feel.

➡ Don't forget to close those chimney dampers if you have a fireplace or stove not in use. An open chimney will send more heat from the house than an open window.

In Summer It's the Heat and Humidity

There's lots you can do to keep cool in the summer. You'll be more comfortable and if you have an air conditioner, you'll be saving energy as well.

Keep an eye out for extra lights burning, particularly incandescent bulbs. They furnish more heat than light and cause your air conditioner to work harder.

An air conditioner's filter should be cleaned or replaced at least once a month. This reduces the load on the unit, thereby decreasing operating costs.

An air conditioner operates most efficiently when placed on the shady side of your house — generally the north side.

Set your air conditioner's thermostat no lower than 78°F, and shut it off when there's a breeze blowing that could cool things off through open windows.

Compare products before you buy an air conditioner. Look for the Seasonal Energy Efficiency Rating (SEER) that you'll find on most appliances today. The higher the number, the more cooling it will produce for a given amount of electricity. Check to see whether it has an Energy Star logo (see box on page 44).

With an air-conditioning unit, bigger isn't necessarily better. A unit bigger than you need for the space to be cooled will make the air clammy and uncomfortable, while a unit too small will just work away burning kilowatt hours and still not cool you.

You'll be more comfortable in summer if you can find ways to lower the humidity — just the opposite of winter, when you're often trying to raise it. The kitchen and laundry areas are moisture-makers, so keep them closed off from the rest of the house as much as possible. Be sure to cover the pots on the stove when you're cooking to save energy and minimize the steam escaping into the room. The covered pot, incidentally, is a good idea any time. It holds the heat in where it will do the cooking, rather than letting it escape into the room. A covered pot will come to a boil faster, saving fuel.

When you take a shower, in addition to turning on your fan, open the bathroom window to let the moisture out.

Since warm air rises, in the summer you'll do well to open the upstairs and attic windows to let the heat escape. Then, in the cool of the evening, let the more temperate air into the house; close the windows first thing in the morning to keep that cool air inside.

Awnings can really be a help in the summer. Particularly on the south windows, awnings will keep the sun away while still letting some light and cooling breezes through. A heavy duck cloth or plastic panels, either in a light color or in white, will be most effective.

A large window fan costs considerably less than an air conditioner and uses a fraction of the power. Perhaps the most effective place to put a fan is in an attic window where it will push the hot air out of the house and draw the cooler air in through the downstairs windows.

For cooling breezes in the spring and fall, open windows from the top to exhaust excess heat without causing drafts that might trigger the thermostat.

You'll be cooler in a minimum amount of loosely fitting clothing. Decorating with bright pastel colors and crisp, cheery plants indoors and out will also help to make your home feel cooler.

Five Easy Ways to Cut Heating Costs

1. Many people can cut their home heating bills by 10 percent or more with one very simple move: Have the furnace cleaned and adjusted properly. If you have an oil burner, that means at least an annual inspection done by a qualified technician.

2. While your oil burner is under discussion, find out whether it is a "conventional" or a "retention head" burner. The latter is much more efficient. It uses smaller fuel nozzles and will save as much as 15 percent on your fuel bill.

3. Forced warm-air furnaces need to have their air filters cleaned or replaced at least twice each winter. A clogged filter chokes off the necessary breathing of the furnace and makes it work harder.

4. When you're rearranging the furniture, make sure that radiators, warm-air registers, or heating units aren't blocked and therefore functioning improperly. If there's an arrangement you *must* have that blocks heat flow, try to let it wait until summer when it won't affect heating efficiency.

5. A little extra humidity permits a lower thermostat setting without discomfort. Try a humidifier, or place pans of water on radiators or a woodstove to put a little moisture in the air.

Chapter ④ ➡ ➡ ➡ ➡ ➡ ➡ ➡ ➡ ➡ ➡

Your Energy-Efficient Kitchen

In many aspects of life, we make it through the day by simply following long-established habits. If we had to think every time about how to brush our teeth, tie our shoes, put on a jacket — well, we might never make it out of the house in the morning. We can do all those things almost without thinking, so they get done smoothly and quickly.

Habits can be ruinous to monthly fuel bills, though, because the inexpensive fuels of the past have led us into some very wasteful practices, particularly in the kitchen. You don't have to drastically change your lifestyle to achieve significant savings, but you'll have to replace some old habits with new, more efficient ones.

Some parts of our lives are optional, but not cooking and eating. What happens in the kitchen is essential, and it happens every day. That's why a careful examination of how fuel energy is used in the kitchen can be vital to your wallet.

Another truth: Because using the kitchen is such an everyday event — and the kitchen is often where much of shared family life happens — developing new habits there may get your family to think about energy use in general, making other aspects of your life more efficient.

Here's an example. We all know it is necessary to put leftover foods into the refrigerator soon after a meal to keep them from turning bad. But there are two ways to do this. One way is to take dishes from the table and pans from the stove and put them directly into the refrigerator in several trips. This way, your refrigerator will be laboring to keep its cool, with all those hot foods and hot pans to chill and the door opening and closing several times.

Opening and closing the refrigerator door is costly. Cold air rushes out as soon as the door is opened. The more frequently the door is opened, the more cold air rushes out.

A better way to clean up after mealtimes is to put the leftovers in storage containers (keep the lids open until cool) and let them sit on the counter for a half-hour or so until they cool a little. Then, all in one operation, they can be placed in the refrigerator for storage.

There isn't much difference between those two methods. It's really no more than exchanging an old set of habits for a new set. Consider, though, that the process takes place in your kitchen several hundred times a year. If it saved you no more than a penny a meal (and it will save more than that) you're looking at a saving of $11 a year just in the way the refrigerator is used after mealtime. Eleven dollars here, 75 cents there, $3 somewhere else — they all add up to make a significant sum, just through a change in habits.

There are, of course, some other ways to save around the house that require investments of time and money. They're worthwhile as well. It may be, though, that simple changes in your habits in the kitchen and elsewhere will save the most of all with the least effort.

Cool Cash Savings

There's money to be saved in your refrigerator. You may be spending more than you need to just by running your refrigerator at a cooler setting than is required. Put an ordinary household thermometer in the refrigerator for a half-hour or so. The temperature should be slightly below 40°F to prevent bacteria from growing, but it doesn't need to be higher.

While you're at it, check the door gaskets all the way around by closing the door on a dollar bill. If the bill slips out easily at any spots, you're wasting money. You may be able to correct the problem by putting strips of thin cardboard behind the gasket where you spot the leak, or by adjusting the latch. If those don't do it, a new gasket is a good investment and isn't hard to install.

Here are some other things to consider: When you stand with the refrigerator door open, thinking about what you'd like to have, you're running up the cost of that snack. Do your best to remember what's inside before you open the door, and then go directly to it. Try to teach your children this habit, too.

Help yourself and your family by putting a checklist on the refrigerator door, listing what's inside and also crossing off what's been eaten. That's the snack menu, and it can save many door openings.

Get organized before meals so that everything you need can be taken out and placed at the ready on the kitchen counter with just one opening of the refrigerator door. Don't forget the catsup.

After coming home from the store, empty all the shopping bags on the counter, put all the items that need refrigeration in one place, and *then* open the refrigerator door.

After dinner, think about storing the leftovers in the way outlined earlier in this chapter, with particular attention to the business of covered containers. This is most important with frost-free models, where moisture is drawn from the foods to condense on the refrigerating coils, causing the defrost cycle to operate more often. If you don't have enough covered refrigerator containers, put the leftovers in cereal bowls and cover with a plate. Don't forget to label your containers; this will keep you from spending time later looking — with an open refrigerator door — for what you want.

Convenient plastic containers can be bought in many stores, but you can also reuse peanut butter jars, cottage cheese containers, and similar packages with lids that can be cleaned to use for storage.

That frost-free feature certainly is a convenience, but a standard refrigerator that must be defrosted by hand a few times a year will use less electricity. When you're buying your next refrigerator, if you really do want the frost-free convenience, look for a model with a power-saver switch. It turns off the defrost heater when humidity is low in the winter and may cut operating costs by as much as 16 percent.

While you're refrigerator shopping, look for an Energy Guide sticker and ask for the manufacturer's information on average annual operating costs. These may vary by as much as $100 a year for the same-size model.

When the kids grow up and have nests of their own, that big refrigerator you once needed may become a liability. A refrigerator operates most efficiently when it's full, and chances are you don't use its full capacity. Consider giving one of the kids the big box and buying a smaller model.

When placing your refrigerator, keep it away from heat producers like ovens and dishwashers. An outside wall is a good idea, particularly if it's a north wall that will tend to be cool both summer and winter.

And be sure there is adequate air space around the refrigerator, to let the motor heat escape readily. If it's been running hot, you could save as much as $3 to $4 a month.

Use Your Freezer Efficiently

Most refrigerators today have a freezer compartment. You may also have a separate freezer or be thinking about purchasing one. Here are some freezer-related economies.

➡ For openers, a freezer will likely be one of your most expensive electrical appliances to operate. A manual-defrost, 14-cubic-foot model will use about 100 kilowatt hours of electricity each month. Multiply your kwh rate (if it isn't shown on your utility bill, call the power company) by that usage to find your cost.

➡ You may use 50 percent more electricity with an automatic defrost model. Weigh that against the modest effort of defrosting several times a year.

➡ Consider your separate freezer as if it were part of a supermarket. Plan your meals for several days — even a week — and transfer the freezer foods to the freezer compartment of the refrigerator all in one "shopping trip."

➡ Keep items that you use frequently, like ice cream and frozen orange juice, in the freezer compartment of the refrigerator so that the big freezer won't need to be opened so often.

➡ Transfer big items like hams, roasts, and turkeys from the freezer or frozen food compartment to the refrigerator at least a day in advance. That way they will thaw gradually and help to cool the refrigerator while they're doing it.

➡ The recommended temperature for frozen foods is 0°F. Put a household thermometer in your freezer and check the temperature. If it's colder than necessary, change the control setting and check again. You may want to set the temperature a little below zero when you are putting away the harvest from your garden or adding many things at once to be frozen. Don't forget to reset it.

➡ Keep your freezer as full as possible. The bulk of the foods will retain the cold better than empty air, making for more economical operation.

➡ Position your separate freezer in a cool part of the cellar, on the back porch, or out in the garage. These are cooler places, particularly during the winter, and your freezer motor won't need to work so hard. Check your instructions to make sure that your model can withstand freezing temperatures without damage.

➡ You'll get extra mileage from your freezer — and your oven — when you cook oversize batches of favorite casseroles and freeze the extra in meal-size packages.

➡ Plan to have your separate freezer empty during the growing season when you're eating fresh foods from the garden. You can then shut it off in summer when it would work the hardest.

➡ Putting frozen foods in well-marked containers and keeping frozen supplies in easily recognized categories will make everything easier to find, lessening the time with the door open while you are searching for something.

➡ A freezer inventory is a good idea. It can be on a sheet of paper or in a small notebook on the wall or on a shelf near the appliance. Menu planning can be done from the inventory, which can even include a locator chart so each item can be found easily. Again, less time with the door open.

➡ Baking a pie? Bake three or four, and cool and freeze the extras. You'll save money by using the oven less, and those frozen pies will be ready weeks or months later for a quick warm-up before going to the table.

➡ Leftover waffle batter? Make the waffles, put them in a plastic bag, and freeze them. They'll perk up almost like freshly made with a few minutes in the toaster or toaster oven.

→ A last — but not least — thought on freezers: The upright models may be more convenient to use, but every time you open the door the cold "falls out." Chest-type freezers are much more frugal in operation.

Cook Quickly and Economically

In China, cooking fuel has been a scarce and expensive commodity for centuries. To solve this problem, the Chinese developed the method of stir-frying food in a wok. Meat and vegetables are cut or sliced into small bite-size pieces and quickly cooked in hot oil. A full meal cooks in minutes. It's tasty, economical, and nutritious, too.

Cooking fuel is also precious in Japan, where tempura cooking has become one of the answers. Again, bite-size pieces of food are cooked in hot oil, but these are dipped in a tasty batter first, quickly fried, and then dunked in one of several appetizing sauces. Another economical treat.

Another way to use the same principle is to cut vegetables into bite-size pieces and cook them in a steamer. They'll cook nearly as fast as in boiling water and will retain more taste and nutrition in the process.

Try to cut back on the number of burners you fire up to prepare a meal. The ideal is something like the pot roast where a complete meal is cooked on one burner. There are many variations, including that all-time favorite, corned beef and cabbage with boiled potatoes.

When boiling water, as for pasta, once the water reaches a boil turn the burner down as far as you can and still maintain the boil. The water is going to get just so hot and no hotter. Too much heat only creates more steam — and wastes more money.

Don't Forget the Oven

Whether it's gas or electric, the oven in a conventional stove is an energy glutton. The problem is compounded if the oven has a preheating feature, and gets even worse if it's the self-cleaning variety.

One route to oven efficiency is to get maximum use when you fire the oven up. For instance, if you plan to bake pies, time it so you can cook dinner in the oven around the same time.

Having roast beef or pork? Try baked acorn squash for the vegetable, with baked potatoes on the side. You can oven-bake the whole meal in one shot.

Do you like mashed potatoes with your roast beef? My mother baked the potatoes; when they were done, she scooped them from their skins and mashed them. After mashing, they went back into the skins with a pat of butter and a little paprika on top, and went back into the oven. Superb.

Casseroles are limited in their variety only by the extent of your imagination. Any time you are baking cakes, pies, cookies, or even a roast, plan to bake a casserole at the same time.

After baking in the winter, leave the oven door open until the oven is cool. No sense wasting that heat. Conversely, in the summer try to schedule some of the baking for the cool of the evening, to avoid overheating the house.

Before putting frozen foods in the oven, thaw them in the refrigerator or in the sink under cold water. They'll cook more quickly, and therefore with less expense.

For desserts and snacks, consider goodies like sliced fresh peaches with milk and sugar, dried fruits, salted nuts, and instant puddings that don't require cooking. Over the course of the year they'll be much more economical than pies and cakes that need to be baked.

A small toaster oven can often be used for single casseroles or individual meals, and it uses less electricity. With that appliance, plus the oven and broiler in your stove, you'll have three choices. Use the smallest that will do the job.

Don't forget to use your slow cooker. It uses much less energy than an oven or stove.

A pressure cooker uses much less fuel than a conventional pan. When you're preparing boiled potatoes, a pressure cooker will use 30 percent less energy, doing the job in half the time.

A microwave oven is even better in that it consumes very little energy. Take advantage of your microwave for at least some part of every meal — you'll see a savings on your utility bill!

Heat Up the Kitchen

The heating units in electric appliances continue to radiate after being turned off. With a little practice you can learn to turn off the heat a few minutes early and finish with the leftover heat.

The kitchen exhaust fan keeps the house cleaner, but in the winter it also pushes precious warm air into the outdoors. Some of the need for the exhaust fan results from the steam and grease spatters caused by cooking at temperatures higher than needed. Cooking at the right temperature can lead to twofold savings.

Retire Some Small Appliances?

Your electric carving knife, electric can opener, mixer, orange juice maker, sandwich grill, and waffle iron are typically used only for a short period of time and do not contribute significantly to your electric bill. However, there are easy, handy alternatives for all those electric appliances that use less power, or no power at all.

Check around for those even less essential small appliances and put them on the top shelf of the closet. Individually they don't use a lot of electricity, but together the electric tooth-brush, electric shoe-shiner, electric car-washer, and the like are unnecessary expenses.

Life-Cycle Costing

When replacing an aging or worn-out appliance, look beyond the purchase price and consider how much it will cost to use the appliance. Two appliances may have similar features but will consume different amounts of energy over their lifetimes. Comparing the life-cycle cost of an appliance, or what it costs over its entire lifetime, is an easy and effective way to figure out which appliance is the most energy efficient.

Look for the Energy Star label when purchasing new appliances. It's a valuable tool to help you identify and purchase products that use less energy without sacrificing perform-ance or design. These products not only save energy; they also help pre-vent air pollution and save money. Appliances with the Energy Star label include refrigerators, dishwash-ers, washing machines, central-air and room air conditioners, lightbulbs and lighting fixtures, boilers, fur-naces, and heat pumps — as well as computers, printers, fax machines, and copiers. The Energy Star label is awarded by the U.S. Environmental Protection Agency and U.S. Department of Energy.

First, estimate how long the appliance will last and its life-time operating cost. The yellow Energy Guide label will indicate the estimated annual energy costs. Finally, add the purchase price and the lifetime operating costs together to get the total life-cycle cost. Also, be sure to check for the Energy Star label.

An example: Refrigerator 1 costs $600 to purchase and $100 a year for an estimated 15 years. Therefore, it's life-cycle cost will be $2,100. Refrigerator 2 costs $700 to buy and $75 a year for 15 years. Its life-cycle cost is $1,825. Even though Refrigerator 2 has a higher purchase price, it is a better investment.

Hot Water
for Less

Hot running water is one of the great inventions of modern civilization. Two hundred years ago only a minority of families in North America had indoor running water. One hundred years ago a minority had indoor hot running water. Today, nearly every home has both hot and cold running water at the turn of the tap.

Now water is becoming more scarce and expensive, and heating it up costs more and more. Fortunately, there are many easy ways to conserve water.

Hot water is important in three areas of the home: the kitchen, bathroom, and laundry. These areas combine to make the water heater one of the major energy consumers in the home, whether it is fueled by oil, gas, or electricity. You may be considering a switch to solar or other alternative-energy sources; chapter 6 will give you some ideas on how doing that can fulfill your hot water needs.

Let's say, though, that you're like most people: Hot water is available at a twist of the wrist from at least three faucets, serves one or more major appliances, and is heated by your heating system or a separate hot water heater. You may already know you have a hot water problem. You're aware of it every time you pay the bills.

By the standards of former times, most of us live like kings. More and more, though, hot water at your fingertips demands a higher price. This chapter is intended to help you scale down the use and cost of hot water. The suggestions given here can significantly change the way you use hot water at your house, but without uncomfortable sacrifice and with substantial savings as a result. Let's get at it!

Dishwashing

Experts disagree on how hot the water should be in the household supply. Some say if you have an automatic dishwasher your water heater should be set at 150°F. Perhaps, if you need something approaching sterilization. Otherwise, even with a dishwasher, 140°F should be plenty hot enough. You can test the temperature with a candy thermometer.

If, however, your hot water heater is set high enough to accommodate the dishwasher, you will waste energy through excessive heat loss. When choosing a dishwasher, look for one with a booster heater. A booster heater raises the temperature of water entering the dishwasher to 140°F; this allows you to set your main hot water heater to a lower setting of 120°F.

Is that temperature important? You bet. Water heating is the second greatest consumer of energy in the home, amounting to as much as 20 percent of the total domestic energy bill. Water heated to more than 120°F will need to be cooled again for almost all purposes, which is wasteful. Turn down the heater thermostat. Each 10-degree reduction in your hot water temperature cuts your water heater's energy use 3 to 5 percent.

Whether you have a dishwasher or do the dishes in the sink, an inexpensive low-flow faucet aerator with a shut-off saves water and energy. You can flip your water on and off without needing to adjust the temperature.

A good supply of certain items will also save fuel. You may not need two dozen pickle forks, but it's a rare household that has too many spoons, coffee mugs, glasses, or bowls. If you constantly run short on these items, buy an additional supply — and you'll run the hot water for dishwashing less often.

What is true for spoons and mugs is also true for saucepans and frying pans. Have some extras of these items, and you'll run the hot water for cleaning a single item much less often.

With a dishwasher, waiting until you have a full load every time is an important money saver. Letting the dishes, pots, and pans pile up in the dishwasher is much more economical than washing them a few at a time.

The most expensive way to rinse the dishes before putting them in the dishwasher is under a running hot-water faucet. Next most expensive is in a sinkful of hot water. Best is in a sinkful of unheated tap water.

If plates are crusted with egg, or a pan has beans burned on the bottom, let the items soak for a few hours in unheated tap water. Nine times out of ten that will do the trick at much less expense than a hot-water soak, or a scrubbing under running water.

When shopping for a dishwasher, look for a model that has the Energy Star label. It will have a switch to cut off the automatic water heater; this can reduce energy consumption by up to 20 percent.

You already have a dishwasher with that feature? Well, when you can, watch the cycle dial. When it gets to the last air-dry segment, just turn it to stop and open the door. In the winter a little extra heat and humidity will be added to the room by this process, and those dishes will dry by themselves quite quickly.

Utensils that are used regularly for nonstaining jobs like heating water for tea don't need to be washed. They can be turned over in a sink rack and left to dry for the next use. Similarly, knives used for clean chores like cutting a grapefruit don't need the whole hot-water cleaning treatment. A quick splash under the cold water faucet and a wipe with a towel will do it. In fact, if you have good knives with riveted wooden handles, that cleaning method is much better for the knife than a hot-water soaking.

The Bathroom

The invention of single-action mixer faucets was a convenience breakthrough but also a serious economy hazard. With that single-spout faucet you get just the water temperature you want and let it run and run. Terrible. It would be better if you still had two separate faucets as older sinks did. Then you'd need to stopper the sink and mix the right temperature in the bowl. You'd save money. With four people in the house, each one using the bathroom sink, say, five times a day, just filling the sink instead of letting the water run might save as much as 40 gallons a day in hot water. That's enough for two full loads through the washing machine, or three quick showers.

That quick shower takes about half as much water as a tub bath. Try to think of soaking in the tub as an occasional luxury, and the quick shower as a frequent necessity. A low-flow showerhead can reduce hot water use by as much as 50 percent. Most people won't feel a bit of difference or will prefer it to the old showerhead.

When you take a tub bath, don't immediately drain the water when you're through. Let the heat from the water radiate into the room until the water is cool. You might even stopper the tub when you take a shower, and let that hot water radiate its heat before it goes down the drain.

Be sure you turn off the faucet all the way when you're finished using the sink or tub. One drop per second from a hot-water faucet is 200 gallons a month, or 2,400 gallons a year.

Cold Water for Laundry?

Consider using a cold-water detergent. Only clothes that are very greasy need water as warm as 80°F to get clean. Your washing machine probably has settings for cold, warm, and hot water. Use the cold for ordinary washing, the warm for very dirty clothes, the hot not at all. By using cold water washing techniques you could save $10 to $15 a month in hot water costs. With today's detergents, cold-water rinsing is fully effective, and the rinse cycles use probably half of the water you use in washing.

Running your washing machine for just a few items? Try to avoid this. Perhaps some necessary items are in short supply. Stock at least a week's supply of the commonplace, most-used items like socks and underwear. It's cheaper to have enough for each person and use the washing machine less frequently.

A larger supply of frequently washed clothes will allow better use of the different washing cycles. Lightweight items such as underclothes, handkerchiefs, blouses, and pillowcases can take a shorter cycle than heavyweights like blankets, jackets, and towels. Make up full, separate loads of the different kinds of washes you do.

What about Your Clothes Dryer?

You've heard the lecture. Do complete loads. Use the most appropriate temperature setting. Keep the lint filter clean. And above all, when purchasing a clothes dryer, look for the model that uses the least energy.

You will need hotter temperatures for some things like baby clothes. Have enough of these, too, so you can make up full loads and make the most of the hot water you use.

When shopping for a new washing machine, look for the versatility of partial-load washing and for the ability to wash at different temperatures. Look for the Energy Star label. Washing machines with this label can use up to 60 percent less energy and 35 percent less water. Be skeptical of overly fussy controls and multiple cycles. All that electronic gadgetry runs with electric current and spins the meter. Once you have figured out which features you need, select the model that uses the least energy.

Six Easy Ways to Cut Hot Water Costs

1. Locate the water heater as near as possible to the places where hot water is used. Water cools as it travels through pipes.

2. Insulate your hot water pipes along the first 6 to 12 feet from the water heater for the greatest savings.

3. Insulate hot-water pipes that travel through unheated areas. Both pipe insulation and wraparound insulation can be bought at most hardware stores and are simple to install.

4. Many new hot water heaters come with adequate insulation. If you have an older model, a hot-water wrap can provide significant savings. Contact your utility company or manufacturer for advice and safety information.

5. The water heater has a drain valve at the bottom. Use it about twice a year, or more often if there is considerable sediment in your water supply. Draining the heater will allow the heating elements to operate more efficiently.

6. Need a new hot water tank or a new heating system? Consider purchasing an indirect water heater. A well-insulated hot water tank connects to the boiler. With its own aquastat to regulate temperature, the boiler will come on much less frequently, which saves energy, especially in the summer.

Chapter 6 ➡ ➡ ➡ ➡ ➡ ➡ ➡ ➡ ➡ ➡

Here Comes the Sun

In the 1970s many people assumed that by the turn of the century most new homes built in the United States would be designed to make effective use of solar energy. Federal energy policies promoted solar energy and conservation and provided tax credits for households that installed solar energy for heating or hot water. Many existing homes were built or retrofitted with various kinds of solar energy devices. This momentum stalled somewhat during the 1980s and 1990s. Hopefully, we will make more progress in the twenty-first century. In any event, the move to solar energy has already begun. Today thousands of homes are fitted with solar energy systems.

Even if the idea of a solar energy system doesn't immediately appeal to you, read on. There are some money-saving ideas here that everyone can use.

To start with, you're already using solar energy. The sunlight that comes in through every window adds to the heat in your home. Unfortunately, at night your heated air leaves through these very same windows. That is why good draperies or insulating window shades are so effective.

The most light, and therefore heat, enters through your south-facing windows. These windows are the most effective solar collectors you can have. I'm not talking about some new invention by which you can make your house look like a space station. I'm talking about plain, old-fashioned windows.

Solar heat is obviously present on every clear day. Not so obviously, it is still with us on cloudy days. In fact, even on a dim day, the hours of daylight have something to offer for reducing your fuel bills.

If you get intrigued with the solar possibilities, there are books and plans available that will take you beyond the scope of this chapter. Here I suggest things you can do right away, at minimal cost and effort, to take greater advantage of that great free source of energy, the sun.

Use Solar Heat — Now

Don't think of solar heat as something for the future, in a new home. Make use of it now. Here are some ways to do it.

➡ Begin on the outside of your house. Black and other dark colors absorb sun warmth; white and light colors reflect that warmth. Assuming you live where it gets cold in the winter, darker colors for your house exterior, particularly your roof, will pass more of the available heat from the sun to your house.

➡ You can get sunburned under water; you can get sunburned on a cloudy day; you can get sunburned through a T-shirt; and you can get sunburned on a ski slope when the temperature is below zero. Naturally, the windows of your house, and especially those facing south, can admit a lot of heat from the sun.

➡ Storm windows will impede the passage of sunlight very little, but they do keep in more of the heat once it has entered your house.

Most conventional greenhouses have glass on four sides and a glass roof. The plants get a lot of light, but the heating bill can be enormous. At night, the heat leaves through the glass walls and roof. A solar greenhouse usually has a large, sloped south-facing area of glass to receive the light the plants need to grow. However, the other sides are well insulated to reduce the heat loss to the outdoors.

➡ In a solar greenhouse, sun heat is stored in the soil and in water containers. At night, this heat radiates into the green-house and keeps it from getting too cold. Take advantage of this concept throughout your house by having solid objects with an ability to store heat standing in the sunlight to store warmth that will be radiated after the sun goes down.

➡ One good heat collector is a windowsill row of flowerpots or an indoor window box. The dirt will store warmth during the day, helping the plants to grow and warming the room at night.

➡ In your house, can the low-lying winter sun slant across the room to warm a brick-fronted fireplace, a slate entryway, or a similar solid surface? Be sure the drapes are pulled back to take advantage of these solar collectors. Don't forget to shut the drapes at night to keep in warmth.

➡ Light-colored shades or slatted blinds drawn across a sunny window will reflect the sun's warmth right back outdoors again. During the daylight hours, keep the sunny windows in the clear to let that warmth in.

➡ The first step into solar power for many people is a solar hot water system. Such systems are available for new homes or for retrofitting on older homes. They will furnish 50 to 100 percent of your hot water requirements. Look at your current cost of heating hot water and talk to a contractor about the costs and possible savings of a solar system. Ask your contractor for references so you can get a better idea of how much people in your area save with their solar hot-water heaters.

➡ If you have unused space up under your roof — and this will certainly be true if yours is a house with a truss-roof design — consult with a plumber on the cost of putting a secondhand, uninsulated hot water tank up there. Make sure your attic floor can support the added weight. At least during the warmer months, the upstairs tank, linked to the water lines before the water gets to your regular heater, will preheat the water, making for less fuel usage for household hot water. If your roof is insulated, that space up top will be warmer than the outdoors even in winter, so the tank up there can pre-warm your water year-round.

➡ Sunshine is not only a source of warmth but also a source of light at the same time. Turning on the light switches in the daytime may be a habit you can break just by rearranging the furniture or opening the blinds more often.

➡ Next time you're ready to repaint or repaper a room, think about how the room is used before you choose the colors. Light colors in a room will bounce the daylight around, making it a pleasant and cheerful place without extra illumination. This is a less important factor in bedrooms, which are used primarily at night.

➡ In fact, in rooms used solely for sleeping the main function windows have is to provide a little ventilation. Wintertime solar heat won't be available when the room is in use, so let the windows be small, or heavily draped.

➡ Window light can be scarce in the kitchen because you often want a lot of storage, rather than windows, on the outside walls. It's even more important, then, to choose light colors for the kitchen walls.

➡ If you're designing from scratch, or doing a major remodeling, think about a combined kitchen-dining area with storage on the north wall and windows on the south and east walls. That way you can have both storage and sunshine.

➡ Whenever possible, place daytime reading and working areas where window light will be sufficient on all but the most overcast days. Specifically, consider the location of the sewing machine, the chair with the magazine rack, the play table for the children, the workbench, and items like an artist's easel or a computer. Light also means heat, so you'll be warmer as you work.

➡ Are you planning to turn a dark attic into a bright living space? A skylight could change a gloomy garret into a pleasant place. Make sure you install a high-quality window or the heat loss in winter will more than cancel out the savings you gain from the daylight. Look for a double-paned window with at least ½-inch air space between each pane. Low-e glass or argon-filled units will reduce heat loss. Some skylights include shades to reduce overheating during the warm months. You can also use the shades, particularly if they are made of a fabric that isulates well, to keep the heat in at night. Finally, select the model with the lowest rate of infiltration.

The Solar Room

Some direct uses of solar energy are available to you. You might consider the sunspace or solar room, a less expensive feature than a full-scale greenhouse.

➡ The solar room will do best on a south wall. The next best choice is an east or west wall, depending on when you use the room and how much the windows are obstructed. It's best to have minimum shading in winter and some summer shade to keep the space cool.

➡ Your solar room will gather heat even during overcast winter days. Look for ways to conduct that heat to the rest of the house, such as a window or small fan.

> Don't forget the simplest solar energy device of all, the solar clothes dryer — also known as the clothesline. It works like a charm and could save you about $50 a year.

➡ The nighttime temperatures in your solar room will be significantly lower than in daytime, so avoid growing exotic tropicals that would require supplementary heat.

➡ Any well-insulated south facing room with a large amount of south-facing glass can provide a wonderful solar-heated space. A back wall and floor in a dark color and of solid masonry — like concrete or stone — will retain sun heat into the nighttime hours. To avoid overheating, minimize skylights and include adequate ventilation.

Chapter 7 ➡ ➡ ➡ ➡ ➡ ➡ ➡ ➡ ➡ ➡

Rake in Savings from Your Garden

Convenience is expensive. Drive down to the supermarket any time of year, even the dead of winter, and you can find fresh vegetables and fruits. Aisles of produce from all over over the world are there for purchase.

To get all this food to your local market requires the expenditure of vast amounts of energy. Petroleum is used to make fertilizers and pesticides as well as the fuel used to power the machines that sow, transplant, cultivate, and harvest. Energy is also consumed during processing, packaging, storing, and shipping. So much energy is used to produce these crops that by the time you finally purchase the food the energy bill often makes up more of the price than the product itself.

The obvious solution: Grow food in your own garden, where it will be just a short walk away from your kitchen table. But unless you grow and preserve food as efficiently as possible, you might not end up saving money or energy at all.

The best way to conserve energy in the garden is to provide optimum growing conditions for the crops you produce. This may seem obvious, but it isn't. Many of the things people do in their gardens not only waste energy, they lower the yield and quality of the crops they produce. A garden that provides optimum growing conditions requires less effort and energy to maintain than a garden that is grown in some of the old-fashioned ways.

Great Soil Can Be Dirt Cheap

The secret to saving energy is efficiency. And when it comes to growing fruits and vegetables, efficiency begins with the soil. Healthy, dynamic soil rarely needs to be tilled because nature tills it for us. Worms and other beneficial soil creatures constantly turn the soil, creating the conditions where plants thrive. Air and water penetrate easily, and nutrients are supplied as the plants need them. What many people don't know is that average garden soil is far from being healthy garden soil. For the best yields with the least effort you need a garden with healthy soil.

Soil is really not much more than sand, silt, or clay mixed with humus, which is decomposed plant and animal material. Average garden soil has plenty of sand, silt, or clay but is almost always lacking in humus. Growing a garden without enough humus in the soil is like playing golf with just one club: You can do it, but it isn't much fun. The easiest way to supply humus to the soil is to feed it compost.

Compost is the name for partially decomposed plant material, like leaves and grass clippings. It looks like rich, dark soil and smells pleasantly earthy. Compost can be purchased if you need a lot of it quickly, or you can make it yourself with little effort. To make your own compost set aside a small section of the yard for the compost pile. Heap grass clippings, fallen leaves, and kitchen scraps into a pile and mix in some manure from grazing animals, like horses or cows. Every few weeks, turn the pile with a garden fork until the compost looks crumbly and dark. When the compost is finished turn it into the garden soil before and after the planting season. During the growing season spread compost beneath your plants for nutrient-rich mulch.

Raising Expectations with Raised Beds

A raised bed is a frame, often of timbers, set on the ground and filled with soil. Raised beds improve soil drainage, allow the soil to warm up faster in the spring, increase soil depth, make the garden more accessible, and encourage higher yields. A raised bed should be wide enough so you can comfortably reach halfway across its width from one side. They can be as long as you want, but most gardeners prefer beds about 8 to 12 feet long. Make the beds from planks of naturally rot-resistant lumber such as cedar or cypress, or from plastic wood. Naturally rot-resistant woods can last for many years before they need replacing, while plastic woods — made from wood fiber and recycled plastics — last for decades but don't leach hazardous chemicals into the soil. Plants grown in raised beds are often healthier and of higher quality than those grown in conventional ways.

Pressure-treated lumber can resist rotting for decades and is a tempting material to use when building raised beds. But most pressure-treated lumber contains chromated copper arsenate (CCA), a compound that is toxic to fungi, insects, and lots of other creatures as well. The vast majority of CCA stays in the wood, but a small amount can leach into the surrounding soil. For this reason wood treated with CCA is generally not recommended for use in raised beds.

Wide Beds Produce More Food

Crops have been planted in single rows for so long that people never ask whether it is the best way to grow vegetables. It isn't. Planting in wide rows is a technique that maximizes growing space while increasing yield and quality. A garden planted in wide rows has space for up to three times as many plants as the same garden planted in single rows. To plant in wide rows, plant a single row following the spacing directions on the seed packet. Now set the second row as far apart as the plants in the first row. For example, if the plants in the first row are 6 inches apart, set the second row 6 inches from the first. Be sure to stagger the rows to give each plant the most efficient use of the allotted space.

Depending on the crop each wide row can accommodate three to six rows of plants. Reduce weeds in walkways between the beds by covering the aisles with a layer of newspaper that is in turn covered with straw. Raised, wide-bed gardens not only produce more food but are also more attractive.

No Till Means No Bill

The combination of healthy deep soil, raised beds, and wide rows not only means higher yields and better quality. It also means you can say good-bye to that old gas-guzzling tiller. These expensive machines are not only unnecessary, they often do more harm than good. Frequent use of tillers damages soil structure and discourages beneficial organisms like worms.

The best gardens use a tiller about twice a year: once in the spring to loosen the soil and once in the fall to turn organic matter into the soil. This means that tillers are best rented or borrowed rather than purchased, and this can save you hundreds of dollars. You will find that the more compost you add to the soil the less tilling it needs to stay loose and easy to work. After a few seasons, many gardeners using raised beds and wide rows find they never use a tiller at all.

Extending the Growing Season

It seems obvious that the longer the growing season the more food you can grow. Short of moving south it isn't so obvious how to easily make the growing season substantially longer. The answer can be found in some old-fashioned ideas updated with a bit of new technology.

Cold frames are simple rectangular structures topped with a glazed lid to let in the sun and hold in the resulting warmth. They used to be made from old windows and planks, but old windows frequently used lead putty to hold the glazing and plank sides blocked the sun. Today's cold frames often have sides and tops made of translucent double-pane acrylic panels that let in the light and insulate much more efficiently than traditional materials. You can even get thermal ventilators that raise and lower the lid as the interior temperature rises or falls.

Hot beds are cold frames that have a contained heat source to warm the soil around the root zone of the plants. You can use electric cables, but they will cost money to purchase and add even more to your electric bill. To make an old-fashioned hot bed, excavate the bed of your cold frame to a depth of 18 inches. Add a 12-inch-deep layer of fresh horse manure to the hole and top with 6 inches of sand. Use a soil thermometer to track the temperature of the sand — it can easily reach 100°F. Set plants in the hot bed when temperature falls below 90°F.

Row covers are thin, lightweight blankets of synthetic, highly insulating materials. They are used to protect crops from cold spells by modifying the air temperature around the plants while keeping frost from forming on the leaves, fruit, and stems. Row covers are usually used with wire hoops that are set into the ground along the perimeter of the garden bed.

The row cover is then draped over the hoops, forming a tunnel. The synthetic fabric of a row cover can be purchased in a variety of weights designed for different conditions. Lightweight blankets protect from light frosts while heavier blankets can protect many plants from even hard frosts.

Greenhouses are expensive additions to the house or yard, but they can make gardening a year-round affair regardless of where you live. Greenhouses can be freestanding structures or can be attached to the house. Freestanding greenhouses come in a wide variety of sizes and are constructed from many different materials. Many are small enough to be set up in a weekend. A small, unheated greenhouse can produce cool-weather crops such as claytonia and winter lettuce even in the middle of a cold northern winter. It also provides a warm, bright environment that can produce transplants of tomatoes, peppers, and other warm weather crops that are as good as or better than anything at the local garden center.

Sunrooms are greenhouses that are attached to the house. They can be used as a greenhouse to grow food and ornamental plants, as well as a passive solar heat source to help warm the house during chill winter days.

Making the Harvest Last

The garden produces food for just a few short months, but people have to eat year-round. One of the secrets to efficient gardening is knowing how to store vegetables so they stay fresh and delicious months after harvest. Some vegetables store perfectly well in a root cellar or similar dark, dry, cool location. Root crops such as beets, carrots, and turnips can be stored in damp sand in a cool, dry spot in the basement. Potatoes and onions store best in baskets in a cool, dry place. Some people believe that braiding onions shortens their storage life. With winter squash and pumpkins, harvest when the stem begins to shrivel. Set the fruit in the sun for a week or so to harden the skins, then place in a cool, dark spot. You can store many types of fruit, such as apples, pears, and quince, under the same conditions as winter squash. They will last for months.

Some vegetables that do not store well, such as beans and corn, can be dried. Beans, peas, and corn can be harvested and dried for a few days, then stored in glass jars. To dry corn, peel back the husks and tie into bunches of about three ears each. Hang the ears in a dry place with good air circulation, such as an attic. The dried kernels can be ground into corn meal or soaked in water and cooked like fresh corn.

To dry beans and peas, spread the pods on a screen in a sunny spot. Once the pods are dried, remove the seeds and place in a dry glass container. Seal tightly until ready to use.

Herbs can also be dried and stored for up to a year after harvest. There are many ways to dry herbs. The old-fashioned method is to harvest the herb, stems and all; tie them into bunches; and hang the bunches from the rafters. This does dry the herbs, but it also allows much of the herb's volatile oils — and flavor — to escape into the air. There are two excellent ways to dry herbs and also retain their fresh taste. The first technique is refrigerator drying. Harvest the herb and place it in a fine-mesh onion bag. Place a refrigerator magnet equipped with a hook on the inside of the refrigerator. Hang the bag of herbs in the fridge and leave it for about a week or until the herbs are dry and slightly crumbly.

A faster method is microwave drying. Set a single layer of herbs on three sheets of paper towels. Place the towels and herbs in the oven and microwave on high for about 30 seconds. Check the herbs to see whether they are dry. Continue to microwave for 15-second intervals until herbs are dry.

Microwave drying works very well for many herbs, but the drying process must be monitored closely as the herbs can easily scorch if zapped too much.

Canning in glass jars can preserve most vegetables that can't be stored or dried. Tomatoes, pickle cucumbers, and string beans are just some of the foods that can be canned. Canning is also a great way to preserve processed foods, such as jellies, jams, tomato sauce, and maple syrup. Store canned foods on shelves in a cool, dry, slightly dark location. Be sure to date each jar so you can use the oldest stock first.

Chapter 8 ➡ ➡ ➡ ➡ ➡ ➡ ➡ ➡ ➡

Fast Facts about Heating with Wood

Historically, when prices for conventional fuels rise, people consider the possibility of burning wood at home. Wood as a fuel source has advantages and disadvantages.

Advantage: Wood is considered a renewable resource. If we plant and harvest it wisely, we can keep using wood without using it up. Getting that down to personal terms, a well-managed woodlot no bigger than 12 acres will provide enough fuel for an average home, every year, forever.

Disadvantage: We know that in many parts of the world wood is extremely scarce. Poor planning and harvesting too frequently can deplete this vital natural resource.

Advantage: Wood as a source of heat can feel so good. It's toasty and homey to sit around a woodstove. After being outdoors on a cold day, nothing feels better than sitting next to a warming fire.

Disadvantage: Wood smoke can contain pollutants that reduce the quality of the air we breathe. Some cities and towns now limit the number of households that can have woodstoves. When buying a woodstove, ask about emissions and efficiency. The catalytic and other stoves of the past 20 years burn much cleaner than older models.

Advantage: Advances in woodstove technology include wood-pellet stoves, which are more convenient to operate and burn more efficiently with lower emissions. These stoves have a longer burn time and are easier to load and control. The fuel for them is usually waste wood that is made into easy-to-handle pellets.

If you have a fireplace, you no doubt enjoy sitting in front of a wood fire. You need to know that a fireplace is an inefficient way to burn wood and requires some managing just to give you a net heat gain. We'll explain that a little later. Even so, a fireplace is a start.

In fact, a fireplace can be a fine start, because it means you have a chimney — one of the essentials for using wood as fuel. A number of good woodstove models are designed to fit on your fireplace hearth and be vented up the fireplace chimney, so if you get at all serious about wood fuel, a fireplace can be a substantial beginning.

It can be helpful to know which are the better kinds of wood to burn. A hickory log, for instance, has locked within it twice as much potential heat as a butternut log of exactly the same size. When looking for fuel efficiency, this kind of knowledge can be very useful, and it's outlined in the pages that follow.

Much wood-burning wisdom goes back to the very dawn of civilization, because wood was humankind's original fuel and, in fact, was the dominant fuel in use in North America as recently as 150 years ago. The tools, equipment, and know-how of using wood fuel are all readily available, both because there are many homes where wood has always been used for heating, and many more that are sprouting shiny new chimneys.

Incidentally, I don't plan to get into the details of wood-stove installation and maintenance, which is the province of other volumes, but I feel compelled to offer one caution. By its very nature, an open fire in your home can be dangerous, and there are particular hazards inherent in the chimneys of fireplaces and woodstoves.

Before installing a stove get some expert advice, or at least start with an authoritative book on the subject. **Be sure to contact your building inspector or local fire department for guidance.** I'd hate to think that your reading of this chapter might create an enthusiasm that would place your home in jeopardy.

With a conventional woodstove, you're going to get some exercise. At the very least, you'll be carrying logs to the fireplace, or sticks to the stove, and later putting the ashes into a bucket or scuttle for removal. You may even be fully managing a woodlot and felling your own trees. How much effort you put into your woodstove will depend on how much time you have and how much energy you have to give.

Every part of the process you do yourself will save you money. Where I live, for instance, a cord of wood split, delivered, and stacked in yard or garage costs approximately $100. It takes about seven cords to heat my house for the winter, so getting my fuel that way could cost $700 to $1000, which would be cheaper than running the oil burner. However, I can cut the same wood on my own land for nothing.

I have bought wood already split; I have bought wood ready for splitting; and I have cut my own. What I do depends in part on my available time when the woodpile needs replenishing. For a cheery fireplace, or a complete wood heat system, you'll likely make your decisions that same way.

Open up the damper and fire the kindling. Here we go!

A More Efficient Fireplace

You have a fireplace? Let's start there.

➡ A fireplace is likely to steal more heat than it delivers. The necessary draft up the chimney pulls warm air from the room, resulting in a net heat loss. This is particularly true as the fire is dying down, radiating less heat into the room but still having a good draft up the chimney.

➡ Your fireplace should have a damper, a gate that closes off the chimney at the throat of the fireplace. As soon as a fire is out and no longer smoking, the damper should be closed. An open fireplace damper will drain heat from a house as fast as an open window.

➡ Glass doors on your fireplace will let you see the flames while minimizing the heat loss from the room. They are particularly valuable after you've gone to bed, because they cut off the heat loss from the room as the fire dies.

➡ Some woodstoves are designed to sit on your fireplace hearth and be vented up the fireplace chimney — an effective idea. Some models have an additional door on the side for firing up the stove while the front doors are shut. Some also have an interior baffle system for greater fuel efficiency. Some allow you to open the front doors and enjoy the open fire. Make sure to use a screen to prevent embers from flying. At all other times, be sure to close the doors.

➡ If you're planning to build an open fireplace, consider including a sheet metal Heatilator box. It will draw in cool air from the floor, warm it around the firebox, and send it warm into the room through vents. By combining it with a glass screen, you can improve your heating efficiency relative to an ordinary fireplace.

➡ Another fireplace accessory is a grate that enhances airflow into and out of the fireplace, thereby increasing heat flow into the room. These grates come in several sizes to accommodate different fireplace designs and can be used with glass doors. A small fan with thermostatic controls can help regulate the heat.

➡ The greatest heat loss from a fireplace is during the night, after an evening fire, when the damper must remain open to let out the smoke. Caution: A slow-burning wood fire is a potential source of dangerous carbon monoxide. Make sure your fire is cold before you close the damper. Covering the fireplace opening with a fire-rated material will cut off the flow of heated air up the chimney.

Wood Facts

The chart on page 76 shows the actual fuel values in various types of wood. The differences are significant. In some parts of North America the fuel woods of lesser value are more readily available, and everywhere pine is easier to cut and split than beech. Get acquainted with what burns best and longest among the woods available where you live.

Here's a fact worth knowing — the actual dimensions of that mysterious measurement, the cord. Many homeowners don't know that a full cord is 4 feet x 4 feet x 8 feet. Because of this, the wood seller can often get away with selling what he loosely calls a cord but what is really precisely what he felt like throwing on the truck that day. Knowing can be saving.

Burning fresh-cut wood will deposit creosote in your chimney and can result in a chimney fire. You'll run less risk and need to clean your chimney less often if you always burn wood that has been cut and split at least 6 months. You can be sure you're burning dry wood when your home supply is stacked at least 6 months before you intend to use it.

Stacking wood in the side yard? Put down parallel poles with the bark still on and stack on top of them. Eventually they will rot, but that's better than having the ground rot eat away firewood into which you've put the work of cutting and splitting. A covered pile will dry faster.

Split Your Own Wood

➡ Think about buying your firewood unsplit. It will be less expensive. Good exercise, too.

➡ Splitting wood on the concrete floor in your basement or garage, or on a brick or stone hearth, is a sure way to ruin your axe, no matter how careful you think you can be.

➡ Some woods don't split well. Birch and maple split beautifully. A piece of gnarled cherry is a tough one. Choose your firewoods carefully if you're going to do the splitting.

➡ Don't try to split long sections of wood before cutting them into stove or fireplace lengths. Short lengths split much more easily.

➡ For splitting firewood, a slightly dull axe is better than one with a razor edge. There's not only less risk of cutting yourself but also less chance of getting the axe stuck in the wood.

➡ Hold the axe handle as near to the end as you can and take a full swing. The momentum of the weight of the axe-head, instead of just your muscle power, will be doing the work.

→ Use an axe whose head tapers out to a flat wedge. A slender head is more likely to get stuck in the log. A double-bitted axe with two blades is not designed for splitting wood. It is dangerous to use and too slender for splitting well.

→ For splitting big, knotty lengths of wood, a maul or a sledgehammer and some splitting wedges will do the trick. A maul looks like a sledgehammer with one side tapered to an edge. Splitting wedges look like fat slices of pie made from tempered steel.

→ If you're going to split a year's supply of fuel wood for your home, consider a power log-splitter. You can probably get one at the tool rental shop in your town. Follow directions carefully.

→ If you have a big, fat stump in your woodpile that looks as if it isn't going to split easily, don't bother trying. That's just the one you need for a chopping block.

→ For sawing trees or full-length cordwood into burning lengths, a chain saw will do the fastest job. Among the hand tools, a bow saw or a bucksaw is the best choice. Cutting firewood with a carpenter's handsaw will wear you out, and chopping it to length with an axe is something you should try only if your doctor recommends an excess of violent exercise.

→ Everyone misses a stroke now and then when splitting wood. Gather up those chips for starter kindling.

→ Birch logs are pretty just as they are sawed from the tree, but they must be split promptly. Birchbark is almost completely waterproof (the native Americans made canoes from it), and unless you split it, the inside wood will rot quickly and get "punky," rendering it useless for firewood.

All of what has just been said about preparing wood for burning applies to stoves as much as it does to fireplaces, and a good woodstove is many times more fuel-efficient than a fireplace at its best.

The Helpful Woodstove

When choosing a woodstove, consider one with a flat top where a pot of water can simmer during the day. This will add needed humidity to your room, and you'll have water for cups of tea or coffee without starting up the cooking range.

Some woodstoves burn wood more efficiently than others. Your stove's workmanship and design are important features that affect efficiency. Make sure your new woodstove has a catalytic combustor or meets Environmental Protection Agency (EPA) emission standards. This increases the efficiency and reduces the pollutants sent into our air. All new stoves are now tested and rated for seasonal and combustion efficiency. Compare efficiencies when purchasing this major appliance. And remember to make sure your stove is correctly sized for the space it will need to heat.

If you'll be using an older stove, look into installing a catalytic add-on to increase efficiency and reduce emissions. If you have a new stove in your plans, consider a wood-burning cookstove. Some models are very attractive, and all have the advantage of saving on kitchen fuel as well as providing room heat.

When starting a stove fire, use rolled paper, slender sticks of kindling, and one or two pieces of split wood. Open all the drafts, get a good fire going, and add more wood when this "starter set" has become a bed of coals. Then adjust the drafts and add more wood as needed when each firing has been reduced to hot coals.

In a well-made, cast-iron woodstove, a few sticks just smoldering on a bed of hot coals will still put out a lot of warmth, and they'll quickly spring to a blaze even after several hours as soon as you open the drafts and add a little oxygen from the outside.

A woodstove is most efficient when installed near the center of the house, on the first floor, or down in the cellar. A stove in the cellar will help keep the water pipes from freezing in a winter emergency.

You can always start a stove fire with paper and well-split kindling. If you can't, check for blockage in your stovepipe draft. Do not use lighter fluid, gasoline, or other flammables to start an indoor stove fire.

You can burn rolled newspapers in your woodstove. One stick of firewood with two "newspaper logs" makes a good combination, and laying this fire is easier than taking the old papers out to be recycled.

If you are using a woodstove regularly, two woodboxes are a good idea: a larger one for the day's fuel supply, and a smaller one to hold kindling splints. Neither woodbox should touch any part of the stove. Dry wood ignites very easily, so keep any woodbox 36 inches from the stove.

It's tempting to use your woodstove as a trash disposal. Don't. It's an unnecessarily risky way to try to save money. In a fireplace or stove, paper trash and other flammables, like Christmas tree branches, burn too hot and with flames big enough to cause a chimney fire. Recycling your paper trash is a much better idea. Artificial logs made of pressed sawdust impregnated with wax or other artificial compounds can also be dangerous. If a fire gets out of control for any reason, artificial logs are almost impossible to extinguish.

A brick wall behind your stove will not only make it safer to operate but will also hold and radiate heat, multiplying your stove's advantages. **Be careful.** Bricks one at a time may not seem particularly heavy, but even a modest brick wall can weigh several hundred pounds. Be sure your floor is braced underneath enough to carry the load of wall plus stove.

Someone taking down a dead tree in the neighborhood may create an opportunity for you. Check with the tree crew. Any part of the leftovers that they'll put in your yard, or let you haul away, can be either kindling or firewood.

Better Wood Burning

Here are some ideas that may make your wood burning easier as well as safer.

➡ Don't have a woodstove exhaust into a flue already in use. Each fire must have a flue of its own.

➡ Yes, it *is* possible to open the drafts on a wood fire and get it so hot it will warp the grates and even the top of your stove. This is most likely to happen when you're trying to get a woodstove hot too fast. Take it easy. Your stove will get up to its best heat in due time. Don't try to force it.

➡ Coal burns much hotter than wood. Don't burn coal in a stove designed for wood.

➡ Clean your chimney at least once a year to keep creosote from building up. The frequency of cleaning depends on the amount of wood you burn and how well it is seasoned. Check the Yellow Pages for chimney-sweep services.

➡ A smoldering fire can lead to increased creosote buildup. This is more likely during the swing seasons — spring and fall — when you don't want an extremely hot fire. A controlled hotter burn from time to time will help reduce this buildup.

➡ Install a magnetic temperature gauge on your flue pipe to help monitor the temperature of your fire.

➡ Insulated, double-wall stovepipe is your best bet for an outside chimney. There will be less moisture condensation than with a single-wall pipe and therefore less buildup of the flammable carbons and tars that cause chimney fires.

➡ A heat exchanger for your woodstove flue pipe will increase the heat output. There are several designs which extract heat from the pipe before the smoke gets outdoors. Some have a fan to blow the trapped warmth into the room.

Final Thoughts on Heating with Wood

➡ Your house design may allow for a small access hatch between the woodpile and your stove or fireplace. That will eliminate carrying wood in from outdoors, with the resulting opening and closing of doors.

➡ Spray a light mist of water on the ashes in stove or fireplace before you remove them to minimize the "fly ash" spreading around the room. Recycle a "spritz" bottle for this job after it is emptied and well rinsed of its previous contents.

CHOOSING FIREWOOD

THE GOOD WOODS

Tree	BTUs per cord (in thousands)
Shagbark Hickory	24,600
Black Locust	24,600
Ironwood	24,100
Apple	23,877
Rock Elm	23,488
White Oak	22,700
Beech	21,800
Yellow Birch	21,300
Sugar Maple	21,300
Red Oak	21,300
White Ash	20,000

SECOND-CHOICE WOODS

Tree	BTUs per cord (in thousands)
Black Walnut	19,500
White Birch	18,900
Black Cherry	18,770
Tamarack (Larch)	18,650
Red Maple	18,600
Green Ash	18,360
Pitch Pine	17,970
Sycamore	17,950
Black Ash	17,300
American Elm	17,200
Silver Maple	17,000

HARDLY WORTH CUTTING

Tree	BTUs per cord (in thousands)
Red Spruce	13,632
Hemlock	13,500
Black Willow	13,206
Butternut	12,800
Red Pine	12,765
Aspen (Poplar)	12,500
White Pine	12,022
Basswood	11,700
Balsam Fir	11,282

Chapter 9 ⇒ ⇒ ⇒ ⇒ ⇒ ⇒ ⇒ ⇒ ⇒ ⇒

Traditional Wisdom That Really Works

Not all that long ago, fiberglass insulation had not been invented, automatic oil burners were still in the future, and tripletrack aluminum storm windows hadn't even been thought about. Just like us, though, people back then wanted to be comfortable at home in the wintertime. Lacking many of the innovations of modern technology that we take for granted, they applied their ingenuity to keeping warm and happy while the wind howled around the corners.

We can be just as ingenious today. In fact, there is considerable overlap between yesterday and today. Many of the ideas in this chapter are drawn from the lives of present-day country people who still practice the arts of their forebears. Why? Because the old ways still work.

Some of the ideas may strike you as quaint or impractical. Then there will be the one that strikes you as both practical and valuable, and you'll try it. I don't intend to present an exhaustive encyclopedia of pioneer arts. Rather, I hope to pique your imagination into some new ways of thinking. Many of the ideas here are quite individual. The ways of one household were not necessarily the ways of another, because the people and the houses were different. The same problems required different solutions.

You and your house are different, too, so consider these ideas not only things you can do but guides to a way of thinking.

You might also consider asking the oldest members of your family about some of the old-time ways. They'll be pleased that you want to learn from them, and you may hear some great old stories with nuggets of wisdom tucked away in them. The old-timers knew how to have a pretty good life without the advantages and the appliances we have today.

Yesterday's Ideas for Today's Savings

➡ Consider the humble footstool. Its real purpose was to get your feet up off the floor where the coldest drafts are swirling around. Place a footstool at each comfortable chair in the living room and you might be able to turn down the thermostat by several degrees.

➡ Keeping your ankles warm contributes greatly to keeping your whole body comfortable. That was the idea behind gaiters, spats, and other ankle-warmers. Try heavy slipper socks for each member of the family to wear in the evening. The kind with leather feet will last longer. Just those warm socks may let you notch down the thermostat a degree or two.

➡ Another ankle-warming idea is to tuck a throw rug at the base of each door leading outside. Even a hardwood door-sill will eventually wear, allowing the chill to seep through when the wind blows.

➡ Another way to combat the floor chills is to bank the foundation of the house. Raw dirt against the house will eventually rot the wooden sills, but loose straw worked well in the older times, and hay bales or bagged leaves are often used in the country today.

➡ You can often identify an older house by the chimney rising through the middle of the roof. The chimney at the end of the house may have some aesthetic appeal, but most of the warmth it holds will be wasted on the outdoors. That central chimney spread all the warmth it could throughout the house.

➡ In rooms with high ceilings, install a ceiling fan. It will circulate the warm air back down to the living space.

➡ In earlier times, people carried a candle or an oil lamp with them from room to room to provide light only where it was needed. We can do something similar today by using lamps and smaller, directed light fixtures. Lighting the individual places where people are reading or working — what is known as "task lighting"— will be less expensive than lighting a whole room with a ceiling light.

➡ Another traditional body-warmer is the afghan. Originally this was a small rug from Afghanistan, and the term came to be applied to different designs of small blankets knitted or crocheted at home. Each well-equipped home had at least one afghan, draped over the end of the couch in the living room and used for keeping the legs warm.

Bed Warmers

We lived out past the end of the power lines for a while when I was young, so winter warmth was achieved old-style. Each of us kids had a good-sized round stone as a personal possession. (You could use a brick.) Each night our stones were heated in the oven of the kitchen range, then my mother would wrap each one in soft flannel and put it in the foot of the bed. Nothing quite like that warm, flannel-wrapped stone to greet your toes as you push down through the cool sheets.

→ When your back is warm, you're likely to feel warmer all over. That's probably why the vest and the sleeveless sweater were invented. Make sure yours is long enough to keep you covered when you bend over or lift your arms.

→ You may have noticed that many of the old four-poster beds were perched on long, sturdy legs rather high off the floor. Well, the closer you get to the ceiling, the warmer it is. There was a practical purpose in that design.

→ Three or four blankets get terribly heavy during the night. One alternative is the electric blanket, but it keeps the meter running. The old-timers counted on a down-filled comforter to keep them warm.

→ The coverlet or bedspread on George Washington's bed was probably more than just a decorative item. It was likely a closely woven, hand-loomed cover made of linsey-woolsey — a mixture of linen and wool. It's a warm combination, particularly when paired with that down comforter.

→ Another old-time favorite was the bed warmer — a covered, shallow brass pan with a long handle. Hot coals from the fire were put in the pan, which was passed between the sheets just before bedtime. The brass bed warmer also worked for roasting chestnuts, and later generations have used it for making popcorn.

→ Today, almost all the shutters you see are purely decorative. Yesterday, they were part of the heating and cooling system. They would be closed on cold winter nights, and those on the sunny side would be closed to keep out sun heat on hot summer days.

➡ That big country kitchen was a homey place. In the winter, it was also the warmest place in the house, so it made sense that the kitchen was big enough for the whole family. Everyone would gather around the lamp in the warm room to finish homework, read, play games, or just munch on fresh cookies and chat.

➡ Many older homes had a summer kitchen added to the back of the house. It had a stove, a sink, and some storage space so cooking could be carried on without heating up the main house. The sink had a drain, but no running water, so there were no pipes to freeze in the winter. Off season, the summer kitchen was used as a storage room.

➡ A cousin to the man's necktie and the woman's fashionable scarf — both relatively useless items of apparel — is that snuggly old item, the shawl. Girls knitted them; grandmothers crocheted them for grandchildren; almost everybody wore them, both indoors and out. They were a handy way to put on a little extra warmth around the neck and shoulders; less cumbersome than a jacket, less likely to muss the hair than a sweater. They were often made of light wool yarns in neutral colors that would harmonize with almost anything. A favorite shawl was a lifetime treasure. Usually wider and lighter in weight than what we would call a scarf, the shawl deserves a revival.

➡ Many older homes had a rack for drying damp winter clothing in front of the woodstove or fireplace. If you are using wood for some of your heat, a rack like this is still a great way to dry soggy mittens or boots, or even to warm up towels before taking a bath.

➡ The old wood-fired kitchen ranges often had a warming oven at eye level. The flue pipe passed through it to give it a moderate temperature. Breads, muffins, rolls, and pies were popped into the warming oven for a little time before serving, and often the dinner plates were warmed there, too — a custom now practiced in fine restaurants.

Chapter 10 ➡ ➡ ➡ ➡ ➡ ➡ ➡ ➡ ➡ ➡

Cut Down on Costly Trips to the Gas Pump

If there is one object that immediately identifies U. S. society, it is the automobile. We're hooked on personal transportation in the form of the private motorcar. Regrettably, automobiles emit large amounts of carbon monoxide and nitrous oxide into our atmosphere, contributing to the greenhouse effect and air pollution. It's unrealistic to think that the automobile will be abandoned any time soon, so we need to find ways to use our automobiles more efficiently.

If you have a car or two, you certainly know about the upward spiral in the cost of petroleum products. You may have considered, or are already driving, a more compact vehicle to economize at the gas pump. Or you may be among the growing numbers of people driving a sport utility vehicle or minivan, in which case you're really feeling the bite out of your budget from higher gasoline prices. Whatever you drive, there are some basic principles to understand when you're trying to cut down your car's fuel consumption.

Your car isn't only toting you from here to there, it's toting itself. The less weight the engine must haul around, the more efficiently it will perform. Therefore, the smaller and lighter the car you can comfortably drive, the less it will cost to operate. Some auto manufacturers have gotten this message, but we still have a long way to go. In the meantime, shop for the most efficient car with the features you need.

The fewer the horses you have to feed to get you from here to there, the less it will cost you. The big twelve-cylinder yachts on wheels that were the luxury cars a generation ago aren't even available today unless you have one custom-built. They revved up a lot of horsepower that wasn't needed.

Change Your Driving Habits

Your driving habits are a key to economical operation of your car. The place to begin understanding those habits is with a miles-per-gallon record that will take the guesswork out of driving economy.

The first place apply that mpg record is in the regular trips you make, such as driving to work. You may be following a traffic flow, or going by what you think is the shortest way, but that may not be the cheapest route. If there are alternative ways from home to job, or to any other regular destination, take the trouble to check them out for mileage efficiency. You may wind up going a new way.

The reason an alternative route may be less costly is that your car operates most efficiently at a steady speed. If the shorter route has lots of stops and starts it probably will require more gas than a longer route that lets you keep an even pace.

The other way to get there may have fewer stoplights. Good. With your engine idling you'll burn a gallon of gas in 50 minutes, going nowhere. Lots of zero mpg waiting at traffic lights and stop signs can be expensive over the course of a year. Have the right change ready at toll booths on your way for minimum waiting time.

Know How to Start Your Car

On most cars you don't have to step on the gas pedal before you start the car. If you must pump the gas pedal several times, something is wrong — have a mechanic look at it.

For the most economical driving in any car, feed just enough gas to maintain momentum at a steady speed. Build up that momentum in as relaxed a way as you can, consistent with the traffic flow. That means easy starts away from your driveway, away from the traffic lights — every time you are accelerating.

Remember, every time you touch the brakes you are paying to reduce the momentum that cost so much to build up. Watch the traffic signs and ease off gradually instead of heavily using your brakes to get to a slower speed.

Tailgating — driving too close to the guy in front — puts your driving pace at the mercy of another driver's whims. As a tailgater you'll be alternately braking and pumping gas as you respond to the forward driver's perception of the road, which is different from yours. Tailgating is not only hazardous, it's expensive.

A quick jab at the gas pedal, or pumping the pedal, squirts pure gas — which should be mixed with air by your carburetor — into the engine's combustion system. Trying to get started, you can flood your engine. A smooth, steady pressure on the gas pedal is always a money-saver.

When you're approaching an uphill climb, use this money-saving technique. Build up a little extra momentum as you approach the base, then keep it steady or even ease off a little as you are climbing. Trying to add speed as you are climbing a hill is one of the most expensive maneuvers you can do. If you're driving a low-horsepower car with standard transmission uphill, be prepared to downshift rather than feed more gas in high gear. It's cheaper.

If you have a choice when you are traveling, make your stops on a downhill slope. Starting from scratch is much cheaper when you're going downhill.

Resist the temptation to coast on a long downhill. In many states this practice is illegal, and for good reason: It's dangerous. When coasting, you don't have the control of your car that you do with the engine engaged. Your brakes can overheat and fade away, you run the hazard of locking your steering wheel in some cars, and you'll save very little gas. When going downhill leave the engine engaged, but take your foot off the gas, or touch the pedal oh-so-lightly.

Make a List and Save Trips

We live about 25 miles from town, so we make a list of everything our household needs before we go shopping.

It's a pain in the neck to get back home and discover we've forgotten something. The household shopping list not only cuts down the number of shopping trips, but also makes it easier to plan the stops on each trip for minimum mileage.

We find that the combination trip is useful. We combine going to church in town with a visit to friends and relations; we schedule a trip to the dentist together with shopping, buying postage stamps, and getting the dog to the vet. With a little household cooperation, you will get more accomplished with minimum mileage.

Ease off on the speed. A car that gets 40 mpg at 40 miles an hour might get as little as 25 mpg at 70. A 10-mile trip flat-out at 60 will take 10 minutes. It will only take 2 minutes longer at 50, and that kind of difference might be used up at a stoplight, or looking for a place to park.

When using air conditioning in the summer, or the heater in the winter, the natural flow of air makes the blower fan unnecessary at more than 40 miles per hour. Since the fan itself can subtract as much as 1 mpg when in use, that's something to consider, particularly on a long trip.

In the winter, start off slowly in a cold car. All lubricants are like molasses for a mile or two. They'll loosen up, and then your engine won't need to work so hard to keep you moving at highway speed. A short warm-up of the engine before starting can also help reduce engine wear, since the first 10 minutes are the hardest-wearing — especially in cold weather.

How to Stretch a Tank of Gas

You can get 6 to 20 percent higher mpg with a properly tuned engine. Keeping a mileage record will tell you when your gas mileage is slipping, which is a signal for a tune-up.

➡ You can easily take care of a few items without going to a service station. One of them is the air filter. A clogged air filter leaves your engine gasping for breath and means you're probably running with a "rich" mixture, that is, more gas and less air. Many department and auto stores carry air filters, and they are simple to change. A clogged air filter can cost you 1 mpg. Replace your air filter regularly.

➡ Dirty oil cuts back engine efficiency, so make sure your oil is changed according to the car manufacturer's recommended schedule. You can change your own, and buying your own oil is much cheaper. There's a drain plug under your engine that will come out readily with a wrench. Have a bucket ready to catch the dirty oil, and remember to dispose of it safely.

➡ If your fan belt is too tight, your engine is working too hard and wasting gas. The belt should give a little to finger pressure when the engine is not running. If it doesn't, you can easily adjust the tension with a wrench.

→ Badly worn spark plugs can cost you as much as 2 mpg. You'll need a special wrench to remove the spark plugs for inspection, and when you get them out you may not know a good one from a bad one. This is probably a job for a trained technician. If you decide to check the plugs yourself, be sure you mark the leads to the distributor cap before taking them off the plugs, so you can get them back on in the proper order.

→ The plugs may need just a little elementary cleaning, which you can do by scraping with a jackknife blade. If one of the plugs looks very different from the others — it's very oily, or blacker, or badly pitted — you should have a trained mechanic evaluate the problem.

→ The car has been a way of life for most Americans. There are alternatives. These include mass transit, bike paths, and car pools. As we develop these alternatives, our need for automobiles will decline and air quality will improve!

Check Your Tires

Your owner's manual has important information on your tires, including the correct air pressure that should be in them. Underinflation of your tires can cost you as much as 1 mpg; overinflation will wear the tires out sooner. You can buy a small pressure gauge and check the pressure yourself from time to time. This method will give you more accurate readings than the air pump at the gas station.

Radial tires have 50 percent less road resistance, so they give you 3 to 19 percent better mpg. They also wear about three times as long, so they're a good buy even though they are more expensive.

Radial snow tires also have less road resistance than conventional winter tires, while still giving necessary road traction.

➡ Heavier cars are more costly to run. A reduction of 200 pounds in automotive weight typically improves fuel economy by nearly 5 percent.

➡ Use the air conditioner in your car as little as possible. It uses a lot of gas. Roll down the windows and get some fresh air!

➡ Using cruise control can save gas. If you drive on the open road often, staying at a constant speed will save fuel.

➡ If you are taking a trip, start early in the day while traffic is light. Plan to stop for meals at times when traffic is heavy.

➡ Don't let your car idle for a long time to warm it up. Also, don't let your car idle for more than a minute after it is warmed up — this idling wastes more gas than restarting your car.

➡ Do not rev the engine and then quickly shut your car off. This wastes gas. It also pumps raw gasoline into the cylinder walls. This can wash away a film of oil that protects the cylinders and will increase engine wear.

➡ The good news is that in the United States since the oil crises of the 1970s, the average car's consumption of fuel has fallen by 50 percent. This is due primarily to more fuel-efficient automobiles.

➡ More good news is that emissions of major urban pollutants have dropped substantially, the result of more complete combustion of fuel and the catalytic conversion of carbon monoxide, nitrogen oxides, and hydrocarbons into carbon dioxide, nitrogen, and water.

Buying a New Car

When you're shopping for a new vehicle, make fuel efficiency a priority. Comparing fuel efficiency is easy because each car has a sticker with estimated city and highway mpg. You should also consider the possibility of purchasing a vehicle that uses both gas and electricity. These hybrid vehicles get a lot more mileage for each gallon of gas and are far less polluting than conventional cars.

Chapter 11 ➡ ➡ ➡ ➡ ➡ ➡ ➡ ➡ ➡ ➡

Tips for an Energy-Efficient Home

Approximately 22 percent of the energy used in the United States is consumed in residences. Most of the energy consumed in homes still comes either directly or indirectly from fossil fuels: oil, natural gas, or coal. These fuels are limited, nonrenewable, and increasingly expensive resources. In the case of oil and natural gas, world supplies could be exhausted in the foreseeable future. Therefore, it is in everyone's best interest to use these precious resources wisely while new energy sources are being developed.

Despite major successes in energy conservation in the last few decades, there is much that we can still do. This chapter contains information on a number of measures that will help you reduce the amount of energy you use in your home, while also making it a more comfortable place to live. Some of the measures may seem trivial, but when added up, the result can be significant energy savings.

These energy conservation measures are largely no-cost or low-cost (less than $10), or moderate-cost ($11 to $50); even the most expensive would probably cost less than $100 to implement. Few require any significant physical alterations to your house. Most require only a change in your energy use habits.

Nationwide, space heating is the largest consumer of energy in residences, and accounts for nearly half of the energy used in a typical household. Water heating accounts for 14 percent; refrigeration for 13 percent; space cooling for 7 percent; and lighting, cooking, and appliances for the remainder.

This chapter will show you how you can reduce the total wattage of lighting in your home while increasing the amount of usable light. It outlines steps you can take to reduce the amount of hot water you use for bathing, dishwashing, and laundering and to make the most energy-efficient use of your appliances.

Caution: Persons over 65, infants, and persons with certain illnesses risk hypothermia if they stay indoors at temperatures less than 65°F. If you think you risk hypothermia by turning your thermostat below 65°F, consult your doctor.

Heating

Nationwide, more energy is consumed to heat homes and houses than for any other purpose, so the largest energy savings can be made in this area. (Note: In some areas of the southern United States, air-conditioning or water heating may account for a larger share of regional energy consumption.)

➡ Thermostats. For homes that have them, thermostats offer the single easiest opportunity to conserve energy, requiring nothing more than setting a dial to the desired temperature. Recommended settings range from 65°F to 70°F for the hours you're active and 55°F to 60°F when you're in bed.

➡ Setback Features. Some thermostats have an automatic setback feature that can lower the temperature around the time you go to bed and raise it again shortly before you get up. See chapter 3 for more information on how to use your thermostat for maximum fuel savings.

➡ Avoid Drafts. Make sure your thermostat is not in a draft. It will sense the cooler air and make the furnace work longer, overheating your home.

➡ Radiator Tips. If your home has radiators they should be kept clean, as dirt and dust absorb heat. Radiator covers should be removed when radiators are in use because the covers absorb heat and block the flow of air through the radiator.

➡ Radiator Types. There are two types of radiators: steam and hot water. In general you should adjust your radiator's steam or hot-water valve only to turn it on or off. Positioning the valve in between does not regulate heat but strains the pipes. If your home is too hot, don't open the window and let the radiator continue to pour out heat. Instead turn the valve all the way off until the temperature in your home is comfortable.

➡ Bleed Radiators. To operate most efficiently, a hot-water radiator must be completely filled with water. At least once a year at the start of the heating season, your radiators should be purged of trapped air. Do this by opening the bleeder valve on each radiator. The bleeder valve is the small valve located at the top and on the end of the radiator. Some bleeder valves can be opened with a screwdriver; others are opened with a key available at hardware stores. When the valve is opened, any trapped air will escape with a hiss followed by a flow of hot water. Once water begins to escape close the valve immediately. Throughout the heating season, bleed radiators that are running cooler than normal.

➡ Air Vent Valves. If your home is equipped with steam-type radiators it is important to check air vent valves each heating season. This vent allows air to escape so that steam can enter the radiator. The valve is usually a small chrome-plated device mounted on the top of the radiator at the end opposite the steam valve. This valve should always be standing straight up with the vent hole at the top. The vent hole must be kept free of dirt and paint for the radiator to operate efficiently.

➡ Radiator Reflectors. Radiator reflectors are usually made from a thin bubble-pack material with aluminum or another shiny substance on one side. Placed on the wall behind the radiator unit, they reflect heat back into the room instead of allowing the heat to seep through the wall or nearby window. They are a moderate-cost item available from hardware stores.

➡ Build It Yourself. You'll spend even less money if you build your own reflector. Obtain a piece of cardboard or insulation board and cut it to cover an area of wall slightly larger than that covered by the radiator. Cover one side of the board with aluminum foil or some other reflective material. Then fasten the reflector to the wall behind the radiator. Whether you buy or build a reflector, be sure that when installed it does not touch the radiator, because it would then conduct heat into the wall behind it instead of reflecting the heat into the room.

➡ Weatherproofing Doors. A poorly fitted outside door will allow warm air to escape during the winter months. However, there are a number of simple no-cost or moderate-cost techniques for making your door more airtight. Warm air can escape between the door frame and the wall. If this is the case in your home, caulk between the frame and the wall.

➡ Door Sweep. The loss of warm air is frequently greatest under the bottom of the door. This air loss can be prevented by installing a door sweep on the bottom edge of your door.

➡ Draft Guard. A no-cost or low-cost alternative to a door sweep is a draft guard. This is a sand-filled tube of cloth is laid against the bottom of your door. You can buy this product cheaply, but the no-cost way is to make it yourself. Cut a 4-inch- to 5-inch-wide strip from an old sheet, dress, or shirt. The strip should be several inches longer than the gap it will plug. Sew the sides and one end together. Then fill with sand and sew shut. Around the sides and top of the door, weather-strip where the door closes against the frame.

➡ Windows. During the winter pull shut blinds, shades, and draperies on all windows at night and on windows with a northern exposure during the day. Open them whenever the windows receive direct, warming sunlight. Uncover east-facing windows in the morning, west-facing windows in the afternoon, and windows with a southern exposure during all daylight hours.

➡ Weatherproofing Windows. Warm air can leak out between the window frame and the wall. You can stop this type of leak by caulking between the frame and the wall.

➡ Leaky Sashes. Warm air can also be lost between the movable window sash and window frame and between the top and bottom sash in a double-hung window. (The window sash is the panes of glass and the framework into which they are set.) In this case, you can prevent air loss by weather-stripping the movable sash.

➡ Rope Caulk. Rope caulk can be placed over the cracks between the sash and the window frame, and where the upper and lower sashes meet. Most people use rope caulk for only one season, though it can be removed, rolled back up, and stored in a jar until next year. A disadvantage of rope caulk is that you must remove it in order to open the window.

➡ Types of Weather Stripping. You can place plastic, adhesive weather stripping on the window frame, pressing it against the sash. This type of weather stripping will last longer than rope caulk, and you can use the window without removing the weather stripping.

The most durable type of weather stripping is the extruded plastic or V-strip that can be placed between the sash and the frame and between the upper and lower sash. Typically, this weather stripping will last for several years and does not interfere with the use of the window.

➡ Loose Panes. Air can escape around the edges of a loose pane. Caulk or tape around the edge of a loose pane where it meets the framework of the sash. If you have a cracked pane of glass, you can find out whether it is losing heat by holding a stick of burning incense up to it. Is the smoke drawn out the crack? If so, replace the cracked pane, or tape over the crack until the pane can be replaced. Weatherproofing your door and windows will make your home more comfortable while conserving energy and saving you money.

➡ Inexpensive Storm Windows. During the winter months a great deal of heat is lost through the glass in your windows. If your home is not supplied with storm windows, you can purchase inexpensive storm window kits or make your own out of clear plastic sheeting. The sheeting is applied to the inside of the window frame and completely covers the sash. The plastic will stop leaks, and the dead air between it and the window will slow the transfer of heat to the outside.

➡ Buying Plastic Sheeting. The plastic can be purchased by the roll. It should be at least 8 mils thick so that it's rugged enough to last the entire winter. Buy it wide enough to cover your widest window from outside one side of its frame to the other. Estimate the length of plastic you will need by measuring the height of each of your windows from the bottom to the top of their frames and adding their total height.

➡ Applying Plastic Sheeting. You can use a number of methods to apply the plastic to the window frame. These include tape, glue, tacks, and wood strips and nails. No matter how you apply it, make sure that the seal between the plastic and the window frame is airtight. Leave one or two windows free of plastic so they can be opened for ventilation.

➡ Air Conditioner Covers. Window- and wall-mounted air conditioners cool your home even in winter by letting in chilly drafts. If you can't remove the unit and close the window, this energy loss can be stopped with an outdoor air conditioner cover made of tough plastic. An inside cover should be used in addition to or (if you cannot safely reach the outside of your unit) in place of an outdoor cover. Air conditioner covers are low-cost items.

➡ Exhaust Fans. When not in use, a kitchen exhaust fan allows warm air to escape from your home. Inexpensive covers are available for exhaust fan openings.

➡ Furniture Arrangement. Arrange furniture and draperies so that they do not block or obstruct heat vents, radiators, or baseboard heaters.

Air Conditioning

In summer, air conditioners are one of the largest consumers of energy. Here are some tips for using them more efficiently and less frequently.

➡ **Air Conditioner Cleaning.** Check the filter at least once at the beginning of the cooling season. If it's clogged, your unit will run longer than necessary. Clean the filter or replace it — it's an inexpensive item. If you can do so safely, check and clean the condenser coils and fins (the grills or spines on the outdoor side of the unit).

➡ **Temperature Control Setting.** The temperature control on your air conditioner should be set no lower than 78°F. Most window units do not have specific degree markings, so refer to a thermometer placed in a part of the room away from the unit's air flow. Don't set the control to a temperature below 78°F when starting up the unit. It won't cool the room faster, and if you forget to set it to a higher temperature once the room is comfortable, you'll be wasting money.

➡ **Air Conditioner Thermostat.** Don't place lamps, TV sets, or other heat sources near your air conditioner thermostat. Heat from these appliances is sensed by the thermostat and could cause the air conditioner to run longer than necessary.

➡ **Buying a Room Air Conditioner.** Check the Seasonal Energy Efficiency Rating (SEER) and select the model with the highest number for the greatest efficiency. Remember to look for the Energy Star label. Make sure the unit is not too big for the space you need to cool. An oversized unit won't cool your house properly. Instead you will spend more money to be less comfortable than with an appropriately sized unit.

➡ **Dress Cool.** Wear loose, lightweight, light-colored clothing in warm weather. This type of clothing allows air to pass across your skin, evaporating moisture and cooling you.

➡ **Window Fans.** The outdoor air temperature is frequently comfortable, especially at night, but there may be no breeze to bring the cooler air into your home. Buy an outdoor thermometer, and mount it so it's visible from your window. When the temperature outside is comfortable, use a window fan instead of the air conditioner. A fan requires as little as one-tenth the energy needed to run an air conditioner.

➡ **Fresh Air.** If your air conditioner has an outside air control to bring in fresh air, use it without turning on the cooling section. The compressor motor in the unit is the big energy user, not the fan. Be sure to close the outside air control when operating the compressor (cooling position) so that the compressor is cooling only room air.

➡ **Lights, Cooking, Appliances.** In the summer, electric lights, cooking, and the use of appliances such as the washer and dryer generate heat and increase the load on your air conditioner. Keep lights low or off whenever possible. Try to schedule cooking and the use of appliances for the cooler parts of the day. If you must use the oven for a number of hours, shut the kitchen off from the rest of the home and use the kitchen exhaust fan to draw off the heat you create.

➡ **Humidity.** High humidity makes warm air even more uncomfortable, especially when you're active. Reschedule chores that produce moisture, such as floor washing, dishwashing, laundering, bathing, and showering, until cooler times of day or night.

Lighting

Want to slow down that spinning electric meter? Be careful how you use lights in your home.

➡ Use lower-wattage light bulbs. Lower-wattage bulbs should be used in halls, vestibules, and other places where no close-up work or reading occur.

➡ Replace high-use incandescent bulbs with fluorescents. Compact fluorescent fixtures and bulbs are now available for almost all lighting needs. Interior and exterior fixtures, security lighting, and table lamps are some examples. These use about one-quarter to one-fifth the amount of electricity used by their incandescent counterparts. For example, a 15-watt fluorescent bulb produces as much light as a 60-watt incandescent bulb. Even though the initial cost is greater, each fluorescent light will typically save $40 to $70 in energy costs. It will also last about 10,000 hours, or ten to fifteen times longer than an incandescent bulb. Any light that is on more than 3 hours a day is a good candidate for replacement.

This technology is improving rapidly. The light is warmer and more pleasing. It is now more flattering and closer to a daylight radiance. The bulbs come on instantly, and the flickering many people remember is no longer present. More and more products are available, which means you can find the right one for most situations. For example, three-way and dimmable fluorescent bulbs are now available. Check your store for the newer, warm-tone, screw-in light bulbs. Your electric utility company may offer rebates on compact fluorescent bulbs or lighting fixtures.

➡ Did you know that compact fluorescent floor lamps (often called torchères) provide the same light output as the halogen torchères, don't get as hot, and use dramatically less energy? Over the lifetime of the lamp, you can save up to $200 on your electric bill.

➡ In areas of your home that need better lighting it is generally more efficient to use a higher-wattage bulb than a number of lower-wattage bulbs.

➡ Dark walls and ceilings may be dramatic, but they absorb light. Pastels or white on walls and ceilings will give maximum illumination with fewer light fixtures burning in the evening and will make a room pleasantly lit without electricity during daylight hours. A white wall reflects 80 percent of the light that hits it, while a black wall reflects just 10 percent.

➡ Switch Habits. When leaving a room for even a short time, turn off the lights.

➡ Use Daylight. When possible, schedule activities requiring good lighting for the daytime. Place your reading chair near the window. Dirty windows let in less light, so clean windows regularly.

➡ Clean Bulbs and Fixtures. Dirt and grime from cooking, cigarette smoke, and dust obstruct light, so keep bulbs, fixtures, and shades clean. For safety's sake remove bulbs before cleaning your fixtures and dry the fixture thoroughly before replacing. Make sure bulbs are cool before removing.

➡ Lamp Location. Make sure that lamps are positioned so that you can make the most efficient use of their light. If you have a lamp by your reading chair or at your desk, you won't have to light up the whole room.

➡ Lamp Shades. Many decorative lamp shades bottle up light or direct it where you don't need it. Light-colored translucent shades are the best for releasing light. Shades on reading lamps should direct most of the light downward. Remember to keep shades clean to let out more light.

➡ Light-Colored Furnishings. Lighter-colored furnishings, curtains, and rugs reflect light and reduce the amount of artificial light needed in a room.

➡ Safety Lights. Do you leave your lights on when going on vacation? Substitute compact fluorescents for incandescent bulbs in those fixtures that will be on 24 hours a day.

➡ Correct Wattage. Have you installed the appropriate wattage for the task at hand? Often people use bulbs with higher wattage than necessary just because they have run out of bulbs with the desired wattage. A lamp with a 75-watt bulb might provide suitable light with a 60-watt bulb, so keep a variety of bulbs on hand for replacements.

➡ Task Lamps. Task lamps provide direct lighting over desks and other work areas. You save energy when you use them instead of turning on the higher-wattage general lighting in the room.

➡ Long-Life Bulbs. Long-life incandescent bulbs are more expensive and less efficient than standard bulbs of the same wattage.

➡ Dimmers. A dimmer switch allows you to reduce the energy going to incandescent bulbs. A light can be adjusted from bright for reading to a gentle glow for watching TV or dining. Some dimmers require no installation. The lamp is simply plugged into the dimmer, and the dimmer is plugged into a wall socket. Wall switches can also be replaced by dimmer switches. Some compact fluorescents have a dimmable feature.

➡ Timers and motion sensors. If you don't like coming home to a dark home, or you want the added protection of leaving some lights on when no one's home, consider lighting timers, which turn lights on and off automatically. Using timers or motion sensors is much less costly in the long run than leaving your lights on all day.

Water

After space heating, water heating may be the next largest item on you total energy bill. Cutting down hot-water use can be a big money-saver.

➡ Water-Saver Showerheads. These showerheads cut the flow of water by 40 to 60 percent and typically have a water cutoff lever. With this feature you can turn off the water while you lather up. These types of showerheads frequently have settings for different types of spray. Water-saver showerheads are low-cost items that simply screw onto your existing shower arm.

➡ Aerators. Installing an aerator in your kitchen or bathroom sink faucet will reduce the water flow. You'll use less hot water and save the energy that would be required to heat it. The sinks in many modern homes are already equipped with aerators, so check with a plumber or your landlord before trying to install one.

Appliances

➡ Turn Them Off. Don't leave appliances running when you're not using them.

➡ Keep Them in Good Working Order. They will last longer, operate more efficiently, and use less energy.

➡ Be Energy-Conscious when Buying Appliances. Compare energy-use information and operating costs of similar models by the same and different manufacturers. An appliance with a lower purchase price may in the long run cost you more than an energy-efficient model with a higher purchase price. Many types of appliances are required by law to have labels showing estimated annual operating costs.

➡ Special Features. Before buying a new appliance with special features, find out how much energy it uses in comparison to a model without the features. For example, a frost-free refrigerator uses more energy than one that must be defrosted manually. It also costs more to purchase. The savings may make it worth passing up such features.

➡ Use Appliances Wisely. Use the appliance that requires the least amount of energy for the job. Toasting bread in the oven takes three times as much energy as toasting it in a toaster.

Refrigerator-Freezer

➡ A Major Energy User. Unlike most household appliances that are operated only periodically, the refrigerator-freezer operates 24 hours a day, 365 days a year. New York City estimates that more than 25 percent of the general electrical costs in an average city home is accounted for by the refrigerator.

➡ Clean Coils. At least once a year carefully clean the condenser coils of your refrigerator, using either the crevice tool attachment of the vacuum cleaner or a long-handled brush. These coils are located behind or beneath the refrigerator.

➡ Door Gasket. The gasket is the strip of flexible plastic or rubber around your refrigerator door that seals the crack when the door is closed. Dried food can break this seal, so clean the gasket periodically to ensure that the seal is airtight.

➡ Temperature Settings. A temperature of 38°F to 40°F is generally recommended for refrigerators; 0°F is advised for freezers. Follow the manufacturer's instructions, but check these settings by placing a thermometer in both sections.

➡ Contents Arrangement. Food retains cold better than air, so keep units as full as possible but don't overcrowd, so air can circulate freely. For the freezer compartment, stack items tightly. Add extra bags of ice to fill spaces.

➡ Humidity or Power-Saver Switch. Many refrigerators have a humidity or power-saver switch. Its purpose is to control small electric heaters around the edge of the door that stop the door from sweating on humid days. At all other times this heating serves no useful purpose. Keep your refrigerator switched to the power-saving or low-humidity position for most of the year.

➡ Manual Defrost. Frost buildup increases the amount of energy needed to cool refrigerators and freezers, so defrost regularly. Never allow your freezer to build up frost more than ¼ inch thick.

Range and Oven

→ **Cooking.** Use a steamer or pressure cooker if you have one. You'll not only save energy but also preserve the nutritional value of food.

→ **Burners.** If you have a gas range, make sure the flame is blue and cone-shaped by keeping the burner clean and unclogged. You can use a piece of wire or pipe cleaner to unclog burner ports. Keep burner reflectors shiny, and they will reflect more heat.

→ **Pots and Pans.** Use flat-bottomed pots and pans, as they provide faster heat transfer. The pot or pan should completely cover the burner or heating element. A small pan on a large burner wastes energy. Shiny pans and clean reflectors help focus heat.

→ **Turn Off the Range.** If you use an electric range, turn off burners shortly before the recommended cooking time is completed. The heat retained in the element will finish the job.

→ **Leave Lids On.** Food cooks faster in pots and pans with tight-fitting covers.

→ **Oven Habits.** Cook as many dishes together as possible. If one dish calls for 325°F, another for 350°F, and a third for 375°F, set the oven for 350°F. Cut a few minutes off the recipe time for the lower-temperature dish and add a few minutes to the higher-temperature dish.

→ **Don't Preheat.** Preheat only when absolutely necessary and don't preheat for dishes cooked for an hour or more. In any case, never preheat for more than 10 minutes.

- Don't Open the Door. Every time you open the oven door, the oven loses about 20 percent of its heat, so don't keep opening the door to see whether your dish is done before the minimum time given in the recipe.

- Don't Overcook. Use thermometers and timers to avoid overcooking.

- Small Ovens. If you have more than one oven, use the smallest one that will do the job. For example, a toaster oven may cost half as much to operate as a full oven, but will cook or heat small items just as well.

- Use the Range, Not the Oven. Whenever you can, use the rangetop. It uses far less energy than the oven.

- Use an Electric Slow Cooker. It uses heat efficiently and costs less. Invest in a slow cooker and a cookbook and you'll be amazed at the variety of dishes you can make.

- Double Recipes. When cooking or baking, double recipes and freeze half for future use.

- Frozen Foods. Thaw frozen foods (except when package instructions or recipes indicate otherwise) before cooking in the oven. Frozen meats require 20 minutes longer per pound to cook than thawed meat.

- Oven Arrangement. Rearrange oven shelves before you cook, not while the oven is on. Allow at least 1 inch of space around each pan in the oven. When using more than one shelf, stagger the pans for better heat distribution.

➡ Minimize the Use of the Self-Clean Feature. Use the feature only when absolutely necessary. When you do use it, start the cleaning cycle after using the oven to utilize retained heat. Wipe up oven spills regularly to avoid the need for frequent cleanings.

➡ No Foil. Never place aluminum foil on an oven floor. It may block vents and impair air circulation, reducing oven temperature as much as 50°F.

➡ Microwave Ovens. Microwave cooking is much more energy efficient than conventional cooking.

Washer and Dryer

➡ Detergent. Use only as much detergent as recommended on the box. Excessive suds hamper effective washing and often require extra rinsing.

➡ Presoak. For heavily soiled clothing, presoak or use the washing machine's soak cycle to avoid second washes.

➡ Don't Overdry. Overdrying wastes energy, sets wrinkles, and causes clothes to wear out more quickly. If your dryer has an automatic dry cycle, use it to prevent overdrying.

➡ Dryer Venting. Generally, dryers should be vented to the outside to avoid putting excess moisture into your home. However, if you have a dry home and an electric dryer, you may be able to vent the dryer into your home during winter. This will help heat the home and add moisture. Cover the vent with a nylon stocking or buy an indoor dryer-vent kit to prevent lint from escaping into your living area.

➡ Dry Consecutive Loads. Drying your clothes in consecutive loads saves the energy required to warm the dryer up to the desired temperature.

Dishwasher

➡ Full Load. Wait until you have a full load before you use your dishwasher, but be careful not to overload it.

➡ Scrape, Don't Rinse. Instead of rinsing your dishes in hot water before loading them into the dishwasher, scrape them with a sponge or spatula.

➡ Rinse Hold Setting. Don't use the rinse hold setting on your machine. It uses 3 to 7 gallons of hot water each time you use it.

➡ Air Dry. Some dishwasher models have an automatic air-dry or overnight dry switch. If yours doesn't, turn off the control knob after the final rinse and then open the door and let the dishes dry by themselves. This can save you up to 10 percent of your total dishwashing energy costs.

➡ Hand Dishwashing. Rinse your dishes in a sink or dishpan of clean water instead of under hot running water.

Other Appliances

➡ Garbage Disposal. Use only cold water when running your disposal. This saves hot water and solidifies grease, which is then ground up and washed down the drain.

➡ Iron. An iron heats up much faster than it cools, so it saves money to begin by ironing low-temperature fabrics first then working up to those that require the highest temperature. Turn off the iron about 5 minutes before you complete your ironing and use the heat retained in the plate to finish the job.

➡ Reduce Your Ironing Load. By promptly removing laundry from the dryer and hanging it up or carefully folding it, you can reduce the need for ironing. Hang clothes in the bathroom when you're bathing or showering — the steam will often remove wrinkles for you. Buy permanent press fabrics and garments.

➡ Hair Dryer. Towel- and air-dry your hair whenever possible. Running an electric hair dryer for 10 minutes uses the same energy as burning a 60-watt light bulb for 3 hours.

➡ Television. "Instant-on" TV sets use energy even when the screen is dark. This type of set may have a "vacation switch" feature so that you can turn it off for long periods. If not, you can plug your set into a switched socket.

Chapter 12 ➡ ➡ ➡ ➡ ➡ ➡ ➡ ➡ ➡ ➡

Buying a Fuel-Smart Home

The average U. S. family moves from one home to another every 5 years. Considering that some people settle down for much longer periods, it works out that many of us move even more often than that.

It's worthwhile, then, to examine some of the factors you should consider when you're looking for your next house. Maybe you'll be building from scratch; maybe you'll be shopping for a house someone else built — either way, you can look for advantages that wouldn't be practical to build into your present home.

You'll probably get closest to the ideal if you're building from the ground up, so much of this chapter assumes that you will. Even if you're going to move to an older home, you can look for the house you would build if you could.

Often, successful living is the art of compromise. You'll be weighing one set of criteria against another and deciding where compromises must be made. In general, remember that investments in energy conservation result in decreased operating costs. Therefore, even if an energy-efficient house costs more to build or to buy, the total amount you pay each month in mortgage payments and utility bills may be the same or lower. And you will be a lot more comfortable in an energy-efficient home.

And when looking for a new home, you can assess the feasibility of modifying and adapting a house to make daily living more economical. Moving the structure to another position on the land may be impossible. Insulating the walls or attic is easy and inexpensive in many situations.

Let's assume your search is in an area where the seasons include some cold winter months.

Study the Setting

If you're looking at home sites in a hilly area, the best location is on a southeast slope. A little rise to the west will tend to cut the force of the prevailing winds in winter, and the southern exposure will take maximum advantage of the sun for winter heating and will give the best prospects for gardening in the summer.

Having picked an ideal location, you will be best off if the principal windows face south and the structure is positioned on an east-west axis to provide a south-facing roof. Deep overhanging eaves on the south side will let you take maximum advantage of the winter sunlight while shading you from the direct heat of the summer sun.

Broad-leafed trees on the south side of your house will make a cooling shade in the summer, then conveniently drop their leaves and let the warmth of the winter sun through, just when you want it.

A solid windbreak of hardy evergreens to the west of your house, and more on the north side, will be a welcome shield from the winter winds and will shade the house from the sun and the heat of the late afternoon in summer.

A light-colored roof will reflect heat; a dark-colored roof will absorb heat. With a truss roof and extra space above the ceiling, the roof color won't make a lot of difference. If there is usable space under the roof and adequate ventilation available, the dark-roof option will save money during the winter months.

Small windows on the north side will provide summer cross-ventilation and minimum exposure to winter cold. Be sure those north windows are double-glazed or covered with storm windows. Low-e glass or argon-filled windows will reduce the heat that is lost through your windows even more.

A Close Look at the House

If the location and grounds satisfy you, it's time to study the house itself — closely.

The two-story design is far more economical than the extended single-floor plan. The principal heat loss in a house is through the walls and roof, so the less surface area you have, the less you'll spend on heat.

Selecting someone to build your home may be the most significant decision you make. Try to find a builder who is informed about the latest developments in energy-efficient new home construction. Your discussions should include how the house will be framed; how much insulation will be installed in the walls, attic, foundation, and basement ceiling; the type of windows that will be installed; the choice of heating systems; and airtight construction. The more you know, the better your house will turn out.

If you are building your own home, use 2 x 6s instead of 2 x 4s in framing outside walls. This will permit use of a heavier layer of insulation. A bonus is an interesting window option; you can set your windows flush with the outer wall and give yourself deep windowsills indoors, or you can do the opposite for an unusual deep-set window effect from the outside.

Building an airtight home is easier than trying to seal up an existing home. A state-of-the-art home, from the energy perspective, will have extremely low infiltration rates. The builder will use special techniques to install a continuous vapor barrier on the interior walls and ceilings. It will be important for the electrician and plumber to understand the importance of sealing the holes they make. The builder will use a blower door to make sure the house is sealed tightly. At this point, you may want or need to install mechanical ventilation. This will ensure adequate ventilation in every room. Moisture from the kitchen and bathrooms will be vented to the outdoors.

One of the major decisions you may need to make in building your home is what kind of heating system to install.

Year-Round Comfort

The wing we built on the former schoolhouse we live in is half below grade and contains three bedrooms. Their windows are smaller and higher up the wall than they might otherwise be, but since bedrooms are used primarily at night, the size and placement of windows isn't critical. The downstairs bedrooms are easy to heat in winter, and stay cool for summer sleeping.

Because your heating system should last about 30 years, this is a good opportunity to invest in energy conservation. Make sure you compare the installation and operating costs for each system. For example, electric heat is relatively inexpensive to install but more expensive to operate than oil or gas. Select an energy-efficient heating system. There are many recent improvements in this technology. For example, new oil- and gas-fired systems vent directly to the outdoors and no longer need chimneys.

Numerous features will affect the home's overall energy consumption. A house that is planned for energy saving will have an unheated garage, woodshed, or toolshed shielding a west or north wall. The buffer space of those unheated rooms is excellent insulation.

Many contemporary designs locate closets and other storage spaces in the house interior in order to leave more room for windows on the outer walls. The center of the house, though, will be the warmest place in winter and not the most sensible place for storage. Try for a design that puts closets and storage spaces on north and west outer walls, where they can serve as insulators.

Functions that require plumbing — the kitchen, bath, and laundry — should be clustered as close to each other as possible. This is easier in a two-story design. The water and drain lines will be short, which will save money when you're installing them and make them easier to secure in a wintertime heating emergency. Also, short hot-water lines keep the water warmer between heater and faucet.

Rooms that may be unused in winter should not have water lines running through them. Given the absence of water lines, extra rooms with separate thermostats can be shut off when they are not in use. There's a money-saver.

Consider getting along without general, full-room illumination. The wall switches at the room entry can be wired to turn on outlets where individual lamps are plugged in.

Where full-room illumination is needed as, perhaps, in the kitchen or playroom, get acquainted with the varieties of fluorescent fixtures. The cool tubes use just one-fourth the power of incandescent light bulbs and are available in warm color tones that are much easier on the eyes than they used to be.

Give a thought to chimney placement. The central chimney will radiate warmth whenever the heating unit is in use. If you are planning to use one or more woodstoves, be sure your house design allows for easy chimney placement.

A final consideration:

Think about the sun when you buy or build. You may not be able to build or buy a solar home now, but will the design or orientation of the house you are thinking about adapt to solar installation at a later date? If the principal roof area is facing south, you're on the way to solar hot water, space heating, or electricity.

Converting Measurements to Metric

The most important metric conversion for this book — and probably the trickiest — is converting Fahrenheit degrees to Celsius. Here's how: Take the given Fahrenheit number, subtract 32 from it, and multiply the result by 5/9. For example, to convert 70°F:

70 – 32 = 38, and 38 x 5/9 = 20°C

For other measurements in this book, use the following chart.

METRIC CONVERSIONS		
WHEN THE MEASUREMENT GIVEN IS	TO CONVERT IT TO	MULTIPLY IT BY
miles	kilometers	1.6
inches	centimeters	2.54
feet	meters	0.305
gallons	liters	3.785
pounds	kilograms	0.45

Index

T

Thermopane windows, 19

Thermostat settings, 25–28, 31, 92, 98

Tillers, use of, 60

V

Vapor barriers, 15, 18, 21, vi

Vegetables, storage of, 62–64

Ventilation, providing for, 17–19, 23

W

Walls, insulating, 19–20, 23–24

Warm-air registers, 34

Washers and dryers, 48–50, 56, 108–9

Water conservation, 45–46, 103

Water heaters
  money-saving ideas, 50
  settings for, 46
  solar systems, 53–54

Weather stripping
  for doors, 2–4, 18–19
  types of, 9, 96
  for windows, 4–7

Window frames, weatherproofing, 7, 95

Windowpanes, weatherproofing, 5–6, 96

Windows
  applying plastic sheeting, 9–10, 96–97

solar collectors and, 51, 52, 54–55

weatherproofing, 4–7, 95

See also Storm windows

Winter fuel efficiency
  and air infiltration, 7–8
  checking exterior doors, 2–4
  checking exterior foundation, 10–12, 79
  checking windows, 4–7
  need for, 1–2
  storm windows, 8–10, 19, 52–53, 98–99

Wood, heating with
  advantages and disadvantages, 65–67
  choosing firewood, 76
  fireplaces, 66, 68–69
  fuel values in, 69–70
  splitting firewood, 70–72

Wood-pellet stoves, 66

Woodstoves
  advantages in, 34, 65–66
  considerations in, 72–74
  installation of, 67

Helpful Web Sites on Being Fuel Smart

The Alliance to Save Energy
www.ase.org
Activist information, tips for consumers, lesson plans for educators, fact sheets, and more.

Federal Energy Regulatory Commission
www.ferc.fed.us
Press releases, speeches, congressional testimony, meeting schedules, listing of associations and regulated entities, key contacts, searchable phone directory, important regulations, and more.

Home Energy **Magazine Online**
http://hem.dis.anl.gov/eehem/index.html
Analysis of energy-efficient technologies for the home.

Office of Energy Efficiency (Canada)
www.oee.nrcan.gc.ca
Consumer information, a guide to business and industry agencies, a listing of workshops and special events, and more.

Oil.com
www.oil.com
A directory for the oil and gas industry plus news by continent, engineering updates, and information about services and organizations.

United States Department of Energy
www.doe.gov
A public reading room as well as information on key people, current news items, the Office of Science Education, upcoming events, and more.

World Energy News
www.worldenergynews.com
Energy news related to politics, environment, science, health, entertainment, and more.